D1572019

GURU

My Days with Del Close

GURU

My Days with Del Close

JEFF GRIGGS

Ivan R. Dee

CHICAGO   2005

Library of Congress Cataloging-in-Publication Data:
Griggs, Jeff, 1971–
    Guru : my days with Del Close / Jeff Griggs
        p. cm.
    Includes bibliographical references and index.
    ISBN 1-56663-614-0 (alk. paper)
        1. Close, Del, 1934– 2. Actors—United States—Biography.   3.
Griggs, Jeff, 1971– I. Title.

PN2287.C5465G75 2005
792.02'8'092—dc22
[B]
                                                      2004056009

Contents

Preface: Improv

Improvised drama *(commedia dell'arte)* is believed to have begun in the fourteenth century in Italy. For some two hundred years, groups of roving comic performers in this tradition traveled from town to town throughout Europe. Instead of relying on a formal script, masked characters worked within a framework of "scenarios," which helped them with entrances and exits as well as defining who would play particular roles. Otherwise they were free to invent their own dialogue and action. Besides playing farce, their popular performances satirized the authority figures of the day.

American improvisational theater can be traced to the 1930s, when Viola Spolin was teaching dramatics to children and adults at a WPA recreational project at Jane Addams's Hull-House in Chicago. Spolin herself had enrolled in the Recreational Training School at Hull-House, where Neva Boyd, a Northwestern University sociologist, used children's games, storytelling, folk dances, and dramatics to stimulate self-expression in both children and adults. This schooling, and her family's love of parlor games, inspired Spolin to use games as an entree into dramatic training. She had decided that children could not be told to "act." Instead she developed structures that bypassed a child's resistance. Her games led a child organically to perform a theatrical task without being directly told what to do.

Spolin's method, still practiced, provides an alternative to American versions of Stanislavsky's famous writings on actor training. The Russian wanted the actor to be motivated by internal needs and desires; the character is the actor's creation. The games, on the other hand, allow character—an extension of the player's self—to emerge spontaneously, as the performer plays with others. The motivation is built in; action is generated not from psychology but from contact with others in space. In reviewing Spolin's work, newspapers of the day marveled at her ability to take an extremely diverse group of people and turn them into actors who actually wrote their own plays.

In the early 1950s, Spolin's son Paul Sills and David Shepherd formed the Compass Theater in Chicago. They used Spolin's games to develop "scenarios," performed for their friends from the University of Chicago. After several incarnations in different cities, the group returned to Chicago and became known as The Second City. It used improvisation to develop sketch material but shied away from using improv as a performance piece in itself. Other groups around the world, however, began using Spolin's games in front of an audience. Still another group of performers believed it could use the method in its purest form by improvising full-length productions.

Del Close, an early practitioner of improv, fervently believed he was present at the creation of a new art form. He devoted his life to the study and teachings of improvisation as an actor-oriented theater, created and performed without any premeditation. He believed it was as valid as jazz, ballet, or opera.

Del explained improv's universal appeal this way: "It's a game that people can play, men and women, professionals and nonprofessionals, actors and nonactors, on pretty much an equal basis. Being a really good actor does not necessarily guarantee that you will be a very good improviser. Sometimes that's the case, but sometimes it's not the case. Being an actual, complete, hopeless wretched geek in real life doesn't disqualify you from being a solid improviser, either."

That appeal drew Del to improv and drew improvisers to him. He approached improv the same way he conducted his life—in a bizarre, dark, and dangerous fashion. Comparing improvisation to the Dionysian festivals of ancient Greece while trumpeting its inherent dangers, he declared, "It's Frankensteinian—an attempt to create a wonderful monster out of our dead bodies! Sure, we need a muse, but we've got to get it under the whip or all hell breaks loose."

His dream was that improv would be considered its own art form. He was a comedian, a director, a teacher, a writer, an actor, a poet, a lighting designer, a fire eater, a junkie, and a philosopher.

He was the Guru.

GURU

My Days with Del Close

1

The Apartment

The first day I was supposed to meet with Del, I picked him up in my roommate's Chevy Cavalier. He lived at the corner of Belmont and Racine in Chicago. I rang his buzzer, and he buzzed me up to his apartment.

The stairwell up to the second floor had a stale smell to it, so I took the steps two at a time. In my head I pictured what his apartment looked like as I climbed higher. I'd heard that he had tons of books, so I imagined there were bookcases with leather-bound volumes stacked everywhere. I fantasized there would be a rolltop desk with mounds of papers with handwritten notes carefully organized. The whole place would be ornately decorated with posters of all the productions Del had performed in and directed.

His door opened as he hollered, "C'mon up and let's see if I can remember what you look like."

I stepped up to the landing and he peered down at me. His hair was sticking up in all directions, his beard was long and tangled. "Oh yes," he grunted, "the Firecracker. I remember you."

I shook my head. "Did you just call me a Firecracker?"

He ignored me. "I made some tea. Come in and talk and we'll see if I'm actually going to go through with this."

I walked up the rest of the stairs and followed him into his apartment.

The smell was the first thing that assaulted me. The stench of cat feces and rotting food permeated the air. Soon the odor of garbage that had been piling up in and around the trash receptacle became the dominating fragrance in the room. There was a strong stench, but I couldn't put my finger on what it was. It instantly took me back to my grade-school days when another student had puked in the seat next to me and the janitor had scattered a pink and blue sandlike substance over the vomit.

I made a conscious effort to keep my mouth closed and breathe through my nose.

The kitchen was the first room I entered. Del poured some hot water into a couple of coffee mugs at the kitchen table. "Those tea bags are still good. I used them earlier today."

I sat in a chair and tried to find a clean place to rest my elbow. There was half-eaten food and crumpled newspapers all over the table. Del put the tea in front of me, where it remained untouched during my entire visit.

"I was telling Charna that I've structured my will so that she gets everything after I die. She said she would rather have me alive and be poor than have me dead and be rich. So she's bitching at me to change my lifestyle a little bit. She wants me to go with you once a week to the bank and the grocery store and maybe we'll grab something to eat while we're out. Do you think you can manage that?"

Charna Halpern was Del's partner at the ImprovOlympic in Chicago. He was the brilliant, precarious, and mystical prophet of improvisational acting, and she was a talented businesswoman and producer. With Del's genius and Charna's business savvy, the two of them had constructed a wildly successful theater and training center.

I scanned the apartment as Del talked. The room to the south was filled with books, but there were no shelves to be found. Two chairs sat in the middle of the room. In the alcove between the kitchen and the living room was Del's brand new thirty-two-inch TV. It was on a cart so that he could turn it around and watch TV in his kitchen or his living room.

"She's hired someone to come in here and clean the place up every once in a while, but they haven't come yet. Or maybe she was planning on you doing that too. Did she mention that she wanted you to do that?"

My heart skipped a beat as I continued to look around. East of the kitchen was the bedroom. There was an uncovered mattress on the dusty hardwood floor, and a single rumpled top sheet lay next to it. A dingy, bare pillow lay on the floor nearby.

I shook my head. "We're just supposed to run errands together. Somebody else is doing the cleaning." I really had no confirmation of this. All I knew was that there was no way in hell I was cleaning up that mess.

In exchange for getting my classes free at the Improv-Olympic Training Center, Charna had drafted me to take Del on his weekly errands. He was in poor health, which made it too difficult for him to carry things. He even had problems making it up stairs. Earlier Charna had helped him with all these things, but as the theater became more successful, she had less time to assist Del with some of his everyday obstacles.

I was chosen to help Del because Charna thought I wouldn't be scared of him. I could be a bit mouthy, and she figured it would be less difficult for him to intimidate me. Not impossible, just less difficult. Del Close scared everyone. He was an intimidating, frightening man.

All of a sudden a breeze blew through the apartment and the mystery smell returned. Del seemed unfazed by it all. Surely it must drive him insane to have all these odors wafting around him like this, I thought. I realized my mouth was open. I closed my mouth quickly, but it was too late. Something rank had snuck in. I held back a gag.

I felt something in my hair and jumped. I turned around and met Scruthers, Del's new cat. I'm not particularly fond of cats, but I'd never been so happy to see one. I was sure that whatever had touched my hair was a rodent.

Del rattled on about how he had come to acquire the cat. In mid-story he stood up and walked behind me into the bathroom. Without skipping a beat in his story, he unzipped his pants and relieved himself without shutting the door. Finishing his business, he zipped up his pants and walked directly to the front door, ready to leave.

It just occurred to me what the mystery odor had been. Unflushed urine.

He opened the door. I stood up and motioned toward the bathroom. "You forgot to flush."

He gave me a stern look. "You in charge of my personal hygiene as well?"

I shook my head. "If I am. I'm leaving. That's too much work for one man. You need a whole team of people to take on that task."

He tried to look angry, but he chuckled as he walked to the bathroom and flushed the toilet. "So I guess you're expecting me to shower before our weekly visits."

"I don't know that it's me so much as it is society in general that would like you to shower before our weekly visits." We headed down the stairs.

Del adjusted his black beret as we walked outside toward my roommate's car. I heard him mumble something that sounded like "fucking smart-ass," but he wouldn't repeat it when I asked him to.

We drove to Treasure Island on Broadway, near Halsted, where Del marveled at the food selection. He had mentioned in the car that he wanted to go somewhere where he could get some specialty foods. I made a stab that Treasure Island would be the best place.

We stood in the bread section as Del looked for pumpernickel. Not just any pumpernickel. He wanted it dense, hard even. There were so many different kinds of pumpernickel. He finally found a small loaf that looked like textured cardboard. Del would make a certain noise when he was extremely happy, and every time he made it I knew I had steered him in the right direction. The noise was a cross between an owl and a monkey.

"Hooo hoo hoo hoo. This is *it*. This is fucking *it*," he chortled. "Let's test it," he announced. He held the loaf high over his head and fired it toward the ground at maximum speed. The sudden launching of the bread startled a small blonde woman and her child, and they ducked behind the stacks of pineapples.

I picked up the pumpernickel to see if he'd made a dent in the floor. This was a hard loaf of bread.

"When I was in Paris, there was this café I went to. I'd sit and order a whole loaf of bread and tea, and I'd sit there and smear caviar all over the bread and eat it while I watched the people pass by. Do you think they have caviar here?" he asked me.

I started to lead Del toward the middle of the store, but he grabbed my arm. His face contorted and turned red as his eyes bulged. He lurched forward, and I could see the muscles in his neck straining to push out a cough. His emphysema was so bad that he couldn't walk twenty steps without having an attack. He just couldn't breathe and couldn't catch his breath. I stood there as he squeezed my arm, trying to regain control.

I locked my knees so I could catch him if he fell. I could manage to keep him from falling too hard, but I wouldn't be able to hold him up for long. He was a big man with extra weight packed on. He had the build of a wide-shouldered man with a trim figure, but age had added some serious pounds to his body. At the age of sixty-two he weighed a solid two hundred thirty.

"Do you want me to call an ambulance?" I asked.

"No," he choked, "I just need a few minutes."

After what felt like an hour, but was actually more like three minutes, he began breathing normally. He set the bread down on the nearest shelf he could reach and grabbed a stray cart sitting nearby. He leaned on it, using it like a walker to move down the aisle. "Let's go home," he said.

"Don't you want to get your bread?"

"I just want to go home," he answered.

We drove the Cavalier back toward his apartment. Just before we got there he turned to me, cocked his eyebrow, and spoke in his deep bass voice, "You would have been in some deep shit if I had died on your first day of taking me out to run errands!"

I laughed. "I know. I was going to blame it on one of the teachers at ImprovOlympic."

He grabbed my arm and squeezed it again. "Charna cannot know about this. Do not tell her anything. We will have our secrets in this little arrangement we have together."

He insisted that I drop him off and let him walk to his apartment himself. As he headed back in, I wondered if I'd ever see him alive again.

I drove back to Treasure Island and found the pumpernickel bread on the shelf where Del had left it. I searched the store and found the caviar section. I didn't know what kind he wanted, so I bought two. I went back to his apartment building and found the front gate open. Someone walked out of the building and held the door open for me. I left the bag of bread and caviar sitting outside his apartment door and walked back down the stairs.

Back in my own apartment, I stared at the phone. After debating for a while, I called Charna. "I'm not going to tell you why, but you need to call Del," I told her after I finally got up the courage.

Thirty minutes later she called back. "He's mad at you," she said when I answered the phone.

"Because I told you that he had an attack?"

"No," she answered. "He's mad at you because you paid fifty bucks for caviar. He said he would have been happy if you'd gotten him the cheap shit."

I asked if he was feeling okay, and she said he was. She added, "He said he liked you and could tell you weren't scared of him because you made smart-ass comments at him all day. He promised he would shower and clean up a little bit before next week."

Week one was finished.

2

Manhattan, Kansas

Del Close was sometimes called "the most famous person you never heard of." But the famous people you've heard of certainly knew Del. At one point he had probably been their teacher, lover, friend, cast mate, or director. Most likely, though, Del had probably managed to shoot up, smoke, or snort drugs with those famous people. He was an enigma.

John Belushi called Del "his greatest influence" while Dan Aykroyd proclaimed that "he taught us not to be afraid." Bill Murray described Del's discipline as "the most important group work since they built the Pyramids."

Del Perry Close, Jr., was born on March 9, 1934, in Manhattan, Kansas, to Del Perry Close, Sr., and Mildred Madeline Etherington-Close. He was second cousin to Dwight David Eisenhower; a few times during Del's youth, the general had shown up for Thanksgiving dinner at the Close home. Fort Riley, the world's largest infantry base, was just nine miles from Manhattan where Del spent his childhood.

Days after Del was born, the city was struck by a dust storm that was remembered as Black Sunday in Kansas, the worst storm of the depression era's Dust Bowl days. Manhattan was in tornado alley, too.

Del's first appearance on stage was as a troll in his grammar school's production of *Three Billy Goats Gruff*. In front of the audience he deviated from the script, beating up and eating all three of the billy goats. It was his first improvised scene.

Del's father owned a jewelry store; his mother stayed home and doted on their only child. She was, as Del would describe her, "the stereotypical 1940s housewife." Del began wearing eyeglasses at age seven and leg braces soon after as a result of being misdiagnosed with polio. His mother taught him that the best way to exorcise demons was to pretend they didn't exist.

The biggest demon was Del's father, an alcoholic before the word was invented. Del once gave my class a peek into his relationship with his father when he said, "Consider your scenes in improvisation in the same manner of rearing a child. The absolute worse thing you can do in either is to be apathetic. To a child, apathy is a greater abuse than any harm that can be done physically. It's the same with your scene work. Lack of emotion is lethal. It will kill every scene. Love, anger, hatred, lust—all go a long way to show urgency, desire, and caring in every scene." Then he added as an afterthought, "If my father had shown me any of those emotions when I was growing up, maybe I wouldn't have been as psychotic as I am. I would have killed for my father to have been angry at me because that would have showed he had some sort of feelings for me. Indifference is fatal."

To gain his father's attention, Del and his classmates staged occasional practical jokes that caught the town by surprise. Once, Del convinced a friend to shoot a gun at him in the middle of a crowded street, whereupon Del feigned a highly dramatic death. While people ran to get medical help, his friends swooped in and carried him away. Del hid for three days before returning home.

His phony death raised quite a stir in the community. *Life* magazine had called Manhattan "the typical American town"; it wasn't used to this kind of excitement. The local newspaper, the *Manhattan Mercury*, ran a headline announcing "Local Boy Stages His Death."

When Del returned home, his father barely raised an eyebrow. His prank had elicited little response. Mildred Close cried to her son, asking why he had scared her so. He had no answer.

"The notoriety I received from that was addictive," Del told my ImprovOlympic class. "From that day on, people were always a little uncomfortable around me. Out of the corner of my eye I would catch them looking at me, and I could tell they were uneasy because they didn't know what I was going to do next."

3

Shower Claws

I could hear the teakettle whistling as I walked into Del's apartment.

"Lookie, lookie. The Firecracker's here," Del said as he sat at the kitchen table. He poured hot water into a couple of coffee cups with used tea bags in them. There was no doubt in my mind these were the same tea bags from my last visit.

Del was soaking wet. Water was dripping from his beard and hair. He'd obviously just walked out of the shower. He hadn't toweled off, either. His black "South Park" T-shirt was sticking to his body.

He also had scratches on his cheek and his forehead.

"Did you cut yourself?" I asked as I tried to ignore the cup of tea in front of me.

He walked into his bedroom and picked up a pair of socks from the middle of the floor. As he walked back into the kitchen he said, "Since you've taken it upon yourself to look after my hygiene, I took a shower before you got here."

Del sat down and put his socks on. They were inside out. I was going to say something about it but decided not to.

"I was feeling sick this morning, so I ran to the sink to throw up and ended up puking all over the cat. I grabbed Scruthers up, took him into the shower, and he scratched the shit out of my face."

I laughed as Del continued. "So then I put on my raincoat and scooped him up and took him back in the shower. He went berserk and scrambled away."

"Where is he now?"

Del pointed, and I saw the cat perched on top of one of the kitchen cabinets. "Little fucker can stay up there as far as I'm concerned."

Del put on his shoes and we headed downstairs to begin our voyage. As soon as we got outside, Del put on his beret and crawled into my best friend's Chevy Nova. I wondered if Del had noticed that we were in a completely different vehicle from our last visit, but he didn't mention it.

Del's bank was all the way downtown. We drove to Rush and Oak, where Del instructed me to pull up in front of the bank and wait for him.

"This is such an illegal spot," I yelled as he walked toward the bank.

"I don't care," he yelled back. "If any pigs come around here and tell you to move, you keep talking to them and stall them until I get out here. Got it?"

He stood at the front door of the bank waiting for me to respond.

I said not loud enough for anyone on the street to hear, "This is the worst bank robbery ever."

For all his ailments and all his deficiencies, Del always had his wit and his hearing. He opened the door wide and yelled back at me, "You gave it away, you fucking twit. Now I'm going to have to shoot somebody."

As Del walked back to the car ten minutes later, he stuck his hands in the air and pretended like he was shooting two revolvers into the sky. Two steps later he had a massive coughing fit, and I thought he'd coughed up a lung. I shook my head. The Wild West was safe today. We couldn't walk twenty feet without our button man needing a nap.

At the grocery store we got Del's necessary items and of course spent twenty minutes looking for his pumpernickel.

"Charna said you were pretty funny in your show last night," Del said as we stood in the checkout line.

"Did she?" I replied.

"Yeah," he said as he leaned against the cart like it was a walker. "She said you were funny, but the show overall was for shit."

The team I was performing with at the time was Monkey Rocket. The funniest part about that team was its name. Actually, the people on the team were hilarious, but as a group we were not. If an audience was looking to watch arguing and bad team chemistry, Monkey Rocket was the team for them.

"What happened?" Del asked.

"I don't know," I replied. "It was pretty bad all the way around. Bad audience."

He cocked his eyebrow and looked at me. "What was the matter with the audience?"

"I don't think they were very smart. They just didn't get it," I answered.

He barely looked at me. He just leaned on the cart and looked forward, staring at the *TV Guide* for sale. "Maybe," he said, "they got it before you did. It's possible that the audience figured it before you did, but by the time you finally spit it back to them they were bored and annoyed that it took you so long to catch up to them." He turned to look at me. "Never blame the audience. They're much smarter than we are. If they didn't like it, it was our fault."

"Audiences come to our theater because they know they aren't simply watching a performance; they're an intricate part of the process. I love for them to give us hyper-mundane suggestions, like wet cardboard so that we can investigate the psychic potential and spiritual depths of wet cardboard. They're expecting us to elevate our intelligence to provide them an ecstatic religious experience."

"You're right," I nodded at him.

"It's not wrong to bomb. Everybody bombs. Just don't bomb and blame the audience."

We moved forward and I piled the fruit juice, cat food, and pumpernickel onto the checkout conveyer.

"Everybody knows the scene and gets the scene. Our job is to get there before everyone else does. Thinking otherwise makes you look foolish."

He was right, and I would remember it. I looked at him and started to laugh. "Just as foolish as a man who thinks he can put on a raincoat in the shower and try to bathe a cat without getting his face scratched."

Del responded, "You fucking twit. Let's rob this grocery store and get the hell out of here."

4

Book Hole

I'd made a mistake.

For the most part, I mapped out my trips with Del so that we would avoid driving by any bookstores. Today, though, we had driven down Lincoln Avenue so that Del could take some posters to be framed. I was unfamiliar with the territory and would be punished for my ignorance.

He must have had some sort of radar inside his head that scanned and discovered obscure, dimly lit, poorly ventilated used bookstores. He never seemed to look directly at the places, he just sensed them. We would be driving along and he would be rambling and mumbling about something he watched on television the night before, and all of a sudden his head would cock and he'd scratch and itch at his dirty beard.

"Turn around, Firecracker," he'd rumble. "I think there was a book shack back there."

He'd never say he saw any of them. He just knew there was one in the vicinity.

Any time we were in a foreign area, I would break out in a sweat and dart my eyes back and forth. I would drive at a pace slow enough to let me scout out the territory in front of me but fast enough to let me accelerate and fly by any book hole that we'd suddenly come upon. Sometimes I would feign interest in whatever television program he was droning on about just so I could ask him a question and jam his radar at the exact moment we'd pass some secondhand book dive.

Once inside, we would not return to the fresh-smelling world for hours. The mustier, the dustier, the better.

The first time we went to a bookstore, I followed around behind him. There was no method to his direction. He just wandered through the moldy shelves waiting to unearth some scribed treasure that had been ignored or dismissed. It was the hunt. Most of the time he walked away empty-handed, but he found the search exhilarating.

I did not. I was bored.

I grabbed a copy of the most interesting paperback I could find and sat down on the floor in the corner of the store to read as Del scoured around and rummaged through piles of books. After a few moments the sales clerk limped over to me. He was a mousy man, and I could tell he was a little scared of Del.

"You with him?" he asked.

"Yes," I answered. "Don't worry, he's not homeless. He just looks like he is."

The clerk nodded and shuffled away. He returned a few minutes later brandishing a book in his hands.

"Here." He handed me the book. "Read this." He shuffled away again.

Wired was written across the dust jacket. I knew what this was. It was the biography of John Belushi, written by Bob Woodward.

I cracked it open and started to read. The first mention of Del was on page twenty-six. It described how Jim Belushi had found John at Del's apartment after the two of them had been doing cocaine together.

A thumping sound erupted from the corner as a stack of books fell over. I looked up and saw Del scurry away from the pile. We were the only two customers in the store. The clerk was standing at his counter a few feet away from me, so he knew I hadn't knocked over the pile. I was sure, though, that Del would attempt to blame me anyway.

On page fifty-five, Del is mentioned again—Del's initial meeting with John and the influence Del would have on his life.

One hundred pages later I heard Del having a coughing fit one aisle over. After he regained his composure, he walked over and nudged me with his foot. "Let's blow this joint," he said as he made his way to the sales clerk's counter.

I took *Wired* with me.

"Sorry the boy knocked down your books," Del apologized to the clerk. "He's slightly retarded."

Del loved to tell people I was retarded. I never argued about it either. I probably should have shaken my head or rolled my eyes to let the people know I wasn't retarded. Instead I'd shrug my shoulders and smile, and we'd walk away.

"What time does the bank close?" Del asked as he threw his books into the back seat of my ex-girlfriend's Oldsmobile Calais.

"Two hours ago," I answered. "The sun was still up when we went in there."

It was fall, so the sun set early. We had been in the book hole for so long that any plans I had for the evening were shot.

I started the car and backed it up to get out of our parking spot. Suddenly Del swung his door open and got out of the car. He walked back into the bookstore with a book in his hand. It was my book. I'd set it between us and hadn't realized he had snatched it up.

Five minutes later he returned to the car. "I told him my little retarded friend had tried to shoplift his book," he said as he
settled in and motioned for me to drive away.

"I paid for that," I exclaimed and reached for the door.

"That's what he said, but I wouldn't hear it," Del said.
"Let's get out of here and we'll just consider it a donation to
your local book shack."

I was steamed. I had just thrown seven dollars into the wind
so Del could continue his childish joke. I should have just gone
back in there and gotten my money from the clerk. Surely he
would know I wasn't really mentally disabled and would give
me my money back.

I shut the door. I couldn't chance it. He wanted me to go in
there so he could follow me in and embarrass me further.

We drove in silence and headed to the pet store for cat
food. Inside, Del once again told the sales clerk I was retarded and added that I had just stolen a book at a used bookstore.

I didn't smile and shrug this time. I just stood there.

The clerk thought we were insane. Actually, she thought
Del was homeless and insane, and she thought I was a thief and
insane.

"Stay here," Del bellowed as we pulled up in front of his
apartment. He took his cat food and books and disappeared
into the shadows of his building.

I sat in the car and debated whether I should leave. I
thought I should just leave and tell him I was too retarded to
know what "Stay here" meant.

Ten minutes later he returned and tossed a book into the
car. "It's an advance copy. He gave it to me months before anyone else saw it."

I picked up the book and saw the title, *Wired*, across the top. It was the same book, but the cover was a little different from the one I had bought in the store.

"You can have it. Take care of it," he said as he shut the door and walked back into the shadows.

The top of the dust jacket was smudged brown from hands that had held it. I opened it and a ten-dollar bill fell into my lap. Inside the cover was an inscription.

"To Del Close

—the real Deep Throat.

Bob Woodward"

5

The Scholar

At Manhattan High School in 1949, Del began culti-
vating the interests that would follow him through his adult-
hood. His love for books and his obsession with science fiction
and the surreal were already entrenched. At the age of fourteen
he co-created the world's first science fiction poetry fan magazine. He was also president of the language club and played
drums for the orchestra.

The summer after his sophomore year, Del enrolled in the
summer dramatics program at the University of Denver. While
there, living with family friends, he had roles in several productions, including a lead character in the Denver Players
staging of *King Henry III*. Returning to Manhattan, he landed a
role in Kansas State University's production of *Macbeth*. He
was a junior in high school.

"I just felt like I was missing something," he told me. "The
whole world was happening around me, and I wasn't doing anything but watching it go by."

Tired of watching, he joined a traveling show that toured
movie theaters throughout the Midwest. He was a stellar student, so he was able to leave school for weeks at a time without
damaging his grades. His initial job for "Dr. Dracula's Tomb of

Terror" was to run through the dark theater throwing cooked spaghetti at the audience when Dr. Dracula announced, "A plague of worms will descend upon you!"

"This voice came from the back one time: 'You call this entertainment? I just shit in my pants.'" Del recalled. He responded to the voice by saying, "Yes, yes I do call that entertainment; I want to squeeze you dry, whether it's of laughter or shit.

"So, y'know, everything since then has been a striving for that."

After throwing fake worms at the audience, Del would make his way to the stage to be the target for the knife thrower. "I quickly realized that getting knives thrown at me was bullshit, so I moved on to something far less dangerous. I learned to eat fire." He called himself Fagstus at first, but changed the name when he realized he was an easy target for ridicule. He became Azrad the Incombustible. Del managed to avoid serious injury in this role. "The only drawback was that several years after I stopped eating fire, food still tasted a little bit like kerosene," he said.

When he finished his junior year of high school at age seventeen, he enrolled at the Kansas State College of Agriculture and Applied Science on a musical scholarship. He stayed there briefly before leaving for Kansas State University.

In the summers Del toured with the traveling show and convinced himself that he wasn't suited for organized education. Each September, as the other students in Dr. Dracula's show headed back to school, Del would persuade himself to try again, and he'd enroll in a new school.

While doing a show in Wichita, Kansas, he stopped at a rare-book auction, eyeing an out-of-print edition of H. P. Lovecraft's *The Mystery of Murdon Grange*. Del bid as much as his budget would allow, but a spirited gentleman carrying a cane and wearing a brown suit eventually outbid him. The two men went head to head again a few minutes later on another Lovecraft book, *The Secret of the Grave*. This time Del got the book.

After the auction the stranger introduced himself to Del. His name was L. Ron Hubbard, an author. Del discovered that Hubbard was trying to complete his collection of Lovecraft's works, so he gave him *The Secret of the Grave*. Hubbard surprised Del by giving him a pendant of a spaceship he was wearing on his lapel.

The two men remained friends, and Del often visited Hubbard. It turned out that Hubbard had written a book called *Dianetics: The Modern Science of Mental Health;* Del was fascinated by his theories. He was also intrigued by the success that *Dianetics* enjoyed.

Del told Hubbard he could make a killing if he capitalized on the spiritual message in the book. According to Del, he told Hubbard, "You could turn this into a religion and get some pretty nifty tax benefits from the government." At Del's urging, Hubbard began exploring the possibility. He went on to create the Church of Scientology.

Del attended the University of Denver for a semester before he moved on to the University of Iowa, where he won a fellowship in the drama and speech department. He lasted only a semester at Iowa before he quit college life for good and moved to New York.

In his one semester at Iowa, Del's roommate was a skinny, wild-haired drama student named Jerry Silberman. Silberman moved to New York after finishing his studies and worked in several Broadway productions before starring in feature films. He had changed his name to Gene Wilder because he couldn't imagine that someone named Jerry Silberman would ever play the role of Hamlet.

Del meanwhile, twenty years old and living in New York, was ready for the lifestyle he had been missing in the Midwest. He considered enrolling in the Actors Studio and studying with Lee Strasberg, but he quickly found the "method" style of acting to be pretentious. And he thought the students and actors of the Actors Studio were pompous and ostentatious.

After playing in a few off-Broadway shows, Del returned to his drums. He enrolled in a music class for the advanced study of all instruments. An excellent drummer, he was often called to fill in for recitals at the Juilliard.

For pocket money, Del reprised his role as Azrad the Incombustible in venues around the city. His fire-eating cemented his reputation as being a little off. He called his cabaret act "resistentialism," his answer to existentialism. About this time he began putting cigarettes out by crushing them on his tongue.

When celebrated Barter Theater in Abdington, Virginia, offered Del an equity contract, he had to wait to join the company until after their first production. Not expecting to be offered a contract, he had already agreed to spend several months in Bermuda as a human torch. While the rest of the Barter company was performing on stage, Del was jumping off a high dive into a burning tank.

Del did summer stock at the Barter Theater for two years. There he met actors Ned Beatty and Mitchell Ryan. Ryan became one of Del's best drinking buddies. Both men believed their carousing was festive and harmless, but they would battle their addictions to alcohol for years to come. Ryan appeared in more than fifty movies and television shows and later became a regular cast member on "Dharma and Greg," playing Greg's wealthy father.

But the most important relationship forged during Del's tenure at the Barter Theater was his friendship with Severn Darden. Darden, an "intellectual" monologist, effortlessly weaved allusions to Freud and Kant into his hilariously nonsensical ramblings. He became Del's closest friend.

When Darden finished his summer stock, he traveled to meet some friends who were moving their moderately successful theater company from Chicago to the Crystal Palace in St. Louis, Missouri. Even though Del didn't have a driver's license, he bought a motorcycle and followed Darden's suggestion to drive to St. Louis to audition for the company.

Actually, Del had auditioned for the same group before joining the Barter. Ted Flicker, who was directing the St. Louis group, had seen Del in an off-Broadway production and recalled his earlier audition. As a result, Del was hired instantly. In 1957 he became a member of the theater group known simply as The Compass.

6

X-treme Detrgnt

We had finished in record time.

We'd visited the bank, pet store, grocery store, bakery, and pharmacy in less than an hour. We weren't rushing. Everything had just gone very smoothly, and all our errands were done.

I'd even managed to nag Del into putting all his dirty clothes into a ten-pound laundry bag. I put the bag in the middle of the apartment and followed around behind him pointing out what should go in. Disgusting, smelly clothes were crammed everywhere.

"You could help, you know," he snapped. He tried to hand me clothes to put in the bag, but I wouldn't touch them.

"I am helping. I'm just not going to touch any of your disgusting clothes."

He threw a shirt toward the bag and cat poop flew in another direction. He looked at me out of the corner of his eye to see if I had seen what had happened.

"Oh my God," I said. "That was gross."

After the bag was full, I walked it over to the cleaners across the street. "Wash these clothes twice," I said to the attendant as I handed her the bag.

"That won't be necessary," she snorted.

As she opened the bag, the odor hit her and her eyes fluttered. She put her hand over her mouth. She closed the bag and wrote on the ticket, "X-treme Cse, X-treme Detrgnt."

I had a feeling they were going to wash it twice.

Del was waiting with tea when I got back. Fortunately I had stopped at the 7-11 next to the cleaners and bought a Pepsi.

I handed Del the ticket for his clothes, and he attached it to his refrigerator with a "South Park" magnet.

We were done.

We stood there for a few minutes, and I could tell he wanted to say something. He had his hands in his pockets and was chewing at his bottom lip.

"What?" I asked.

He shrugged his shoulders. "You want to get high?"

I chuckled and smiled at him. "It's two in the afternoon."

He took his hands out of pockets and ran his fingers through his beard. "You trying to tell me that you've never smoked up in the middle of the day?"

"I'm actually telling you that I've never 'smoked up' at any time of the day," I said.

He was amazed.

"Ever?"

"Never."

It looked like I had taken a frying pan and smacked it against Del's face. He was flabbergasted.

"What are you, a narc?" he asked.

"Yes, Del, I've traveled here from the sixties to bust you and all of your senior citizen friends," I responded.

"Aren't you curious?"

I nodded. "I'm curious. But I'm not curious about what it would feel like to do it. I'm curious about why you want to do it. That type of thing."

"So you're judging me," he growled.

"I could care less. I'm just saying that I'm not going to smoke pot with you."

"Fuck you," he said, rummaging in the cabinet under his sink.

"Why?"

"Because you're standing there judging me."

The top of his body had disappeared into the cabinet as he continued to explore its contents.

I stood there watching him for several moments. I started to ask if I could help him look for whatever he was searching for, but I changed my mind. He crawled out from under the sink.

"Why are you mad at me?" I asked.

"Get the hell out of here. I'm going to smoke my weed, and I don't want my buzz to be clouded by your pissy, self-righteous bullshit."

He found a Tupperware container and set it on the table. There was a clear glass contraption in the middle of the table, and Del took some marijuana out of the Tupperware and packed it into the top of the contraption.

I was fascinated by what he was doing, but I was also annoyed. I'd seen the glass item on the table with water in it, but I didn't have any idea what it was. I had absolutely no desire to smoke pot with him or anyone else, but I was curious to see what he was doing and how he was doing it.

I did not, however, care to stay there any longer. He was acting like a baby. I grabbed my keys off the kitchen table and walked toward the door.

Del sat down and reached for a lighter that was on the table. "Now, if you don't mind, I'm going to smoke my pot. I had enough that I could've shared it with you, but since you don't want it, I'll invite you to shove it up your ass. Of course, I'm sure you won't do that because you're too afraid you'll get a contact high."

"Whatever, Del," I mumbled. He turned his back to me and lit his lighter. I opened the door and left.

"You're a dick," Del yelled after me.

I drove my friend's Mazda back to her apartment and then jumped on the Brown Line and headed home.

I had four messages on my voice mail when I finally got back to my apartment. All of them were from Del.

Message number one: "You, my friend, are an asshole. Fuck you and your judgment. This is Del."

Message number two: "I was just thinking about you and your fucking judgment, and I want you to know that I shit on your judgment and piss on your morals. It must horrify you that you have to spend your afternoons with a junkie like me. You fucking pissant. This is Del."

Message number three: "I'm sitting here and thinking about all of this and relishing in the irony that some day your virginal daughter will be deflowered by a junkie with a hard-on. That is all. This is Del."

Message number four: "I may have overreacted. Call me. This is Del."

I called him. He answered on the eleventh ring.

"I'm a little too high to discuss this right now, but I wanted to apologize for getting so riled up this afternoon."

"I don't care if you smoke, Del. You kind of have a reputation for doing a lot more than that," I told him. I could hear him scratching his beard through the phone.

"Well," he started, "let's just learn from this little experience, and next time I get high I won't kick you out of my apartment."

"That's fine," I replied.

"So we're square?" he asked.

"We're square."

He sighed and there was silence for a little while. This was a petty argument; we both thought the other person was wrong.

In an instant we were back to our regular routine. His mind was foggy, and he wanted me to tell him what channel "Win Ben Stein's Money" was on. I told him, and we chatted for a few moments about how he could try to get on the show.

Just before we got off the phone, he said, "Call me tomorrow and remind me we had this discussion. I'm way too high to remember this."

7

Chris

"You look better," I told Del as we sat in the uncomfortable chairs in the pharmacy area of the Walgreens at Belmont and Halsted.

"I feel better," he nodded, shifting in his seat.

Since my first visit with him, his health and disposition had improved noticeably. After our first trip to the grocery store, I was sure I would walk into his apartment and discover him lying in the middle of the floor.

Dead.

Surrounded by cat feces.

But he was doing all right. He even whistled as we got into my ex-roommate's Chevy Cavalier. It was annoying, and I asked him to stop, but it was indicative of behavior that was beginning to be routine.

"Why are you doing better?" I asked as we waited for the pretty blonde lab assistant to fill Del's prescription.

He smiled. "Frank got me some drugs."

"Legal or illegal?"

"Both." He shifted in his chair again. These were the types of chairs that businesses put out because they were required to. Both of us were shifting around like idiots because neither of us could get comfortable.

Del pushed his glasses up to the top of his substantial nose. "Charna's brother-in-law is a doctor. He gave me a prescription for this antihistamine that I shoot down my throat. It's amazing. I haven't been able to breathe this well in years."

I didn't ask if this was one of the legal or illegal drugs he was talking about.

"The stuff we're getting today," Del added, "helps me so that I'm not so congested. Over the past sixty-odd years I've crammed quite a bit of tar into these lungs."

We had been talking in a nice conversational tone so far, but Del increased the volume several levels so that he could exclaim, "What I'd really like is some nitrous."

He looked out of the corner of his glasses to see if I was laughing. I was not. I rolled my eyes and shook my head.

"Is it too much to ask that the pharmacist spread it around instead of hogging all of it for himself?"

The dozen or so people waiting for their prescriptions shifted uncomfortably. There were six seats, but Del and I were the only people seated.

Besides constantly informing everyone around us that I was retarded, Del also liked to announce himself as a junkie. He had already loudly exclaimed both things to our fellow Walgreens patrons. They wanted to sit down, but they were all way too scared even to attempt it.

Now that everyone was sufficiently frightened, Del picked up the newspaper and began to read it.

I don't know why he had the constant urge to shock people, but he did. He relished it. Earlier, while we were eating at the Golden Nugget, he announced to everyone in the restaurant that the meal was delicious and he was ready to settle back and enjoy a cup of coffee "as soon as the cunt comes back and re-fills the fucking empty cup."

"Jesus," Del muttered as he shoved the newspaper into my hand. He pointed to an article halfway down the entertainment section.

It was about Chris Farley. When Del, after many years of exile, had been asked to come back to Second City to direct "The Gods Must Be Lazy" in 1989, he had demanded the right to handpick his cast. Chris Farley was someone who amused him, so Del immediately snatched him up. Chris went on to star on "Saturday Night Live," and Del solidified his status as an excellent judge of talent.

"I found Del and started following him around," Chris had said about Del. "He taught me to attack the stage."

Del loved Chris's energy and innocence, and Chris responded by worshiping him. According to Chris, Del's instructions to him were basically these: "Try to kill the audience. Fucking kill them. I want you to make them laugh so hard they vomit and choke on their own vomit."

Over the past few years, though, Chris had left SNL and had starred in some truly awful movies. A few weeks earlier I had sat in Del's kitchen and listened to him talk to Chris on the phone about why he had not seen *Beverly Hills Ninja*.

"I'll see your movie, Chris," he said, "as long as you can guarantee that those two wasted hours will be added back on at the end of my life. If you want to take a shit on celluloid and get paid for it, don't expect me to watch it."

I asked Del what Chris's response was, and he said, "Oh, Del. It's only ninety minutes long—wise guy."

"It's safe to say that he didn't get it," Del said to me.

The newspaper had a report of a drunken Chris Farley visiting different bars in Chicago in the wee hours of the morning. It was early December, and Chris had been spotted outside the Excalibur nightclub dressed only in a white T-shirt and boxer shorts.

"Buffoon," Del said and shook his head.

I didn't know Chris Farley, but I felt bad for him.

"How is this different from what you used to do?" I was trying somehow to defend Chris.

"It's much different," Del said. "Everything I did, I did for the experience. Chris is doing it for the acceptance. He thinks he's got to be the life of the party wherever he goes."

It had been rumored that Chris didn't leave SNL of his own accord. We'd all heard that he was asked to leave because of his problems with alcohol.

I mentioned to Del that I was surprised to see all of this because I'd just read an article in *Entertainment Weekly* discussing how Chris had beaten his drinking problem.

Del chewed on his lip and stared straight ahead. "He's doing more than drinking. He's a mess."

I didn't want to hear this. "You think he's doing drugs?" I asked Del.

It was like I wasn't talking to Del at all. He never looked at me, and I couldn't tell if he was hearing my questions when I asked them. He looked forward, chewed his lip, and never changed his emotion.

"I know for certain he's doing drugs," Del said.

We sat there in silence until his medicine was ready.

Seven days later Chris was dead.

I had to work on Thursday, December 18, so Del and I moved our weekly excursion to Friday. Because of my job as a tour guide, I was standing in front of the Hancock Building as the ambulance carrying Chris's body screeched away.

The next day I went to pick up Del, and he didn't want to go. He just wanted to sit at home and watch HBO. On the table sat a *Chicago Tribune*, which had thoroughly covered Chris's death. In one of the articles, Del was quoted as saying, "Chris didn't have to learn how to be honest and intelligent on stage, because he didn't know any other way to be."

Del's anger burst through as he told the newspaper, "There is, in effect, this whole industry dedicated to turning you into your public image. The thing that bothers me is that they assume making a lot of money is going to compensate for this. In the meantime there are tremendous psychic and physical dues to pay. All celebrities and certainly comedians tend to wind up being public sacrifices, and I'm getting tired of it."

I sat around and watched the last hour of *Peggy Sue Got Married* with him. Eventually I decided to go.

Neither of us mentioned Chris until I got up to leave. There was a gift-wrapped package on the table, and Del looked at it for a few seconds.

"I was going to give this to the fat guy for Christmas, but he went and died on me," Del said as he handed it to me. "You can have it." It was a book: *Frame-Up! The Shocking Scandal That Destroyed Hollywood's Biggest Comedy Star, Rosco "Fatty" Arbuckle.*

Several months earlier, Del had told Chris the story of "Fatty" Arbuckle and had encouraged him to develop it into a movie to star in. Chris had expressed a lot of interest in doing the "Fatty" story and had even told reporters and friends it was going to be his next project.

Inside the book Del had written: "Dear Chris—Okay, so it's Cheap! Have a steaming Solstice anyway—Del (Xmas '97)."

The following two weeks were holidays, so Del and I decided to forgo our trips. If he needed anything, he would call me.

I wished him a happy holiday and walked down the stairs.

The door opened, and I turned and looked up toward the third-floor landing. Del bellowed down the stairs, "Don't eat too much and get fat. I'm oh for three with fat, funny guys.

Belushi, Farley, and John Candy—three fat funny guys and all three of them dead." Then he added, "I was pretty fond of that fat bastard." It was quick, it was quiet, and it was devoid of emotion.

I nodded and walked down the rest of the stairs. Del walked back into his apartment and locked the door behind him. When I reached the bottom I could hear him laughing at something on TV.

I made a mental note to remind myself to call Del on Christmas. He would grumble and thank me and tell me he didn't celebrate holidays that promote Jesus, but I knew he'd appreciate it.

I stepped outside into the snow.

8

The Rules

"Just a second there. Please stop what you're doing!"

The words rumbled from inside a fog of smoke emanating from the bar in the ImprovOlympic cabaret. I was on the side of the stage waiting to edit a scene when Del stopped the action.

"Young lady, what is your name?" he asked.

"Caroline," she answered.

"Caroline, do you think you're funny?" he asked.

"I don't know," she stammered.

"Well, then, explain to me what you're doing in this scene," he ordered her.

She was playing an overweight character and started every line with, "I'm so fat . . ." She had affected a plodding walk and a high-pitched voice. I grimaced as she explained to Del that she thought it would be funny to play a fat person.

"Do you have any overweight family members?" Del asked. She informed him that her grandmother and her aunt were overweight.

"Well, I bet your Christmas dinners are a fucking laugh house riot when you see those fat asses walking around. In fact, I would encourage you to do that character the next time you see them and see how they like it."

She was blinking back tears as Del addressed her. Her hands were clenched into a fist, and her knuckles were bright white. The rest of us stood around like statues. The intensity of the moment had us frozen. We were afraid any movement would direct Del's wrath toward us.

"You're so invested in your little mimicry of obese people that you have totally ignored your scene partner. I appreciate the fact that you have initiated with a strong character, but you have completely neglected to become involved in your character's relationship. You need to consciously invest more concern in your scene partner than in yourself so that you can explore all the facets of your existence and environment.

"All you're doing is mocking fat people and thus making a mockery of my stage. You have no relationship, no location, and no purpose to be on stage. I'd like you to remove yourself."

She quickly walked off the stage and sat down. I was closest to the stage, but there was no way I was taking a step onto it. My friend Jackie Rosepal walked to the middle with another classmate, and I said a silent prayer for her.

Jackie started the scene by saying, "I missed you while you were gone."

Her scene partner's name was Darrin. He responded by portraying a mentally retarded character. Darrin answered her by saying, "I want to play with my toys."

"Stop!" Del bellowed.

I walked to the shadows and hid. Del wasn't supposed to be smoking because of his health, but he had picked out some used butts from the ashtray and was smoking them. He stood, and the smoke from his cigarette engulfed him. It looked like he was standing in the middle of a cloud.

My roommate Mike elbowed me and said, "It's like God is yelling at them."

"You're doing exactly what I just yelled at *her* for," Del shouted, exasperated. "This young lady just delivered a wonderful opening line that led the two of you into a relationship, and you completely ignored her so that you could play a fucking retard.

"I'd like to see some goddamn integrity on stage. Are we so incompetent and unenlightened that we can't elevate ourselves to have some sort of dignity when we perform? You have to treat your scene partners like artists and poets. When you lower yourself to play retards and obese people, you pander to the audience and you insult your scene partner, the audience, and me.

"All of these big, broad, ridiculous characters have to stop. You should wear your character like a thin veil. It should be an extension of you. We're interested in creating honest and sincere characters. Those characters will certainly have quirks and blemishes, but we're here to celebrate those, not ridicule the people for having them."

I'd heard this comment before from one of Del's former students, Bill Murray. "I wear my characters like a trench coat," he had declared during an interview promoting *What About Bob?* "That is what Del Close taught. Roles are really you underneath."

Del stopped and returned to his chair beside the bar. Jackie and Darrin stood awkwardly on stage. He hadn't given further instructions, so they weren't sure if they were supposed to return to their scene. She looked at me to see if I knew what they should do, but I looked away. I didn't want her dragging me into this mess.

Del slammed his hand down on the bar and launched into another tirade.

"The insincerity of these characters is astonishingly disrespectful as well. A thousand cheap laughs can never compare to one intelligent chuckle. Don't cheapen yourself or lower yourself to get a laugh. The laugh will come out of respect, not out of contemptuousness. Which would you rather be known as, the village idiot or the artist with the insightful intellect?

"To receive a laugh, you must understand where it comes from. Years ago I came up with the definition of laughter, and it still rings true today. It will be true for millions of years to come. Laughter is a response to a gestalt formation where two previously incompatible or dissimilar ideas suddenly form into a new piece of understanding. The energy release during that reaction comes out in laughter."

He paused and waited for us to catch up with him. He was flying a thousand steps ahead of us, and we were desperately trying to keep up. He was used to that—and not just with students. The actor and director Harold Ramis once said, "He had always been possibly a century ahead of his time. There was no hope of catching up with Del, but he took us to new places spiritually and in consciousness that none of us had been before."

Once Del was satisfied that we understood him, he continued. "To gain respect and to succeed in this art form, you must play to the height of your intelligence. You can play an idiot or a retard, but strive to play the smartest retard that you possibly can. Improvisers often play drunks or retarded people as an excuse to be dumb. If you're playing someone drunk or stoned or retarded, allow them to be strong, motivated characters."

Del motioned for Jackie and Darrin to resume their scene, then launched into a coughing fit. His body lurched forward, and he grabbed the chair in front of him. The gurgling sound of the phlegm in his throat was unsettling. His coughing attacks were difficult to watch. I always looked away so I didn't have to observe them, but my roommate Mike stared as if he were witnessing the Hindenburg explode. On his face was a mixture of horror, fear, and amazement.

One of the students poured a glass of water and handed it to Del while he was in the middle of the attack. Once it had subsided, he yelled, "Why the hell does everyone bring me water every time I start coughing? I don't breathe water. Just for once, I'd like for someone to get me a fucking tracheotomy tube."

He lit up another used cigarette butt and motioned for the performers to start again. He insisted they maintain the aspects of the scene as they had started before but play it with a heightened awareness of their intelligence. Jackie repeated her first line, and Darrin played her mentally challenged husband. He kept trying to tell her that he loved her, but he kept getting distracted by her shiny keys.

Midway through the scene, Del stood up and walked to the bathroom. The action on stage stopped. Darrin and Jackie looked around, asking if they should continue. No one knew what to do. If he had wanted us to stop he would have instructed everyone to freeze for a few minutes. On the other hand, how was he going to critique the scene if he was in the bathroom during its key parts? The bathroom door swung open and Del walked back into the cabaret. "Why did you stop?" he bellowed. "Did I tell you to stop? What's going on here?"

"We didn't know if you wanted us to continue," Jackie answered.

"I was just taking a piss. If I had needed to shit, the improv would have ceased," he answered. "Finish your scene." Del sat in his seat and lit his last used cigarette butt. Jackie continued her scene, and class finished thirty minutes later.

As we filed out of class, Mike, Jackie, and I discussed the brilliance Del had bestowed on us. The two most important rules being: Del does not breathe water! Improv ceases for Del's bowel movements!

We had learned our lessons from the master.

9

The Compass

With the Compass Players in 1957, Del discovered the performance medium that would become an obsession for him and influence the remainder of his life.

The Compass Players developed sketch comedy from improvisation games and performed it cabaret style. The crew drew its humorous content from its community, reflecting the problems and circumstances of society through comedy based on real life. The improvisation games were based on Viola Spolin's work.

Viola's son, Paul Sills, along with Bernie Sahlins and David Shepherd at the University of Chicago, had formed the Compass Players in the late 1940s. The Chicago version of the troupe had imploded because of personality conflicts and financial struggles. The cast scattered throughout the country, and different Compass theaters soon began to experiment with this new form they had created.

St. Louis was the first Compass Players theater to open outside Chicago, and Del was a member of that first cast. In Chicago the performers had specialized in "scenarios": the plot and direction of the scenes were worked out ahead of time, but the dialogue changed each night.

Sills, Shepherd, and Sahlins produced the St. Louis version, but they were also busy in other parts of the country and in other aspects of their lives. So they gave explicit directions as to what they wanted in the performances and left everything else to the performers and the director, Ted Flicker.

Flicker and the cast soon began throwing aside the idea of using improvisation as a tool or technique to produce performance material. They started using improvisation as an actual performance piece.

The idea of improvising and inventing a new show every night was just as mind-boggling to Del as it was to the audience. Del felt like he was a trapeze artist flying without a net. "We were leading a vanguard crusade that challenged the intelligence and creativity of each of the performers as well as the members of the audience," Del said. "We were exploring facets of our minds that had been dormant throughout our entire lives.

"We stood on the precipice of revolutionizing theater as we knew it. Improvisation had not only taken on the state of being an art form but had also begun to feel like spiritual enlightenment. As a group, we elevated each other to a state where we were collectively thinking on multiple levels while engaging in a gestalt intelligence that was leading us into directions we would never have explored on our own.

"It was intoxicating, the feeling of euphoria we felt on those nights we were improvising. The audience was taking the ride with us. We had broken down the fourth wall and asked them to become part of the process we were building."

Besides Del, the St. Louis cast included Severn Darden, Mike Nichols, Elaine May, Nancy Ponder, Ted Flicker, and, for a short time, Jo Henderson. They agreed to guidelines and rules when they first began to improvise. After weeks of nightly work, they began to evolve theories and styles from their successes and failures. It was in St. Louis that the most important rule of improv was discovered: "yes and."

"We would watch all these scenes devolve into conflict and could see the audience becoming disinterested and bored," Del said. "We determined that in order for improvisation to succeed as art or theater or comedy, we had to avoid finding conflict—'yes but'—in our scenes. Instead we had to invite the characters to develop an understanding and appreciation of each other—'yes and.' We weren't encouraging each other to be namby-pamby, fake-happy all the time, but we discovered that the scenes where the characters avoided conflict and worked with each other instead of against each other were far more interesting."

Del's vast knowledge and acerbic wit astounded the St. Louis audiences. He took chances, pushing audiences and fellow cast members to levels and limits they'd never expected.

Experimentation was not limited to the stage. Del tried drugs for the first time while performing with the Compass. The group seemed determined to experience every chemical substance available. St. Louis was in the midst of urban renewal, so old pharmacies were being torn down and their equipment and bottles sold to antique stores. The cast would frequent antique stores to get their drugs, buying half-full bottles of opium and morphine.

Del also became romantically involved with Elaine May, falling in love with her talent and ability. She was brash and bold, and Del was smitten.

Mike Nichols was a different situation. Nichols and May were already an established comedy team that had toured and performed on television and theaters around the country. He and Del never got along, and Del's relationship with Elaine put even more distance between the two men. Nichols represented the upper middle class that Del had resented and spent his life rebelling against.

While their shows were a big hit with audiences, they weren't enough to sustain the continuation of the St. Louis version of the Compass Players.

Less than a year after its debut, the St. Louis company closed its doors. But what had happened theatrically in those few short months would last for years to come.

Improvisation as a theatrical performance piece was born. An art form had been discovered, and Del Close had found a lifelong passion.

10

Pogo the Clown

I sat in the driver's seat of my friend Jackie's Ford Taurus as Del stepped into the bank. We were about done with our errands, and I was ready to be finished. I was in a bad mood.

A couple months earlier I had met a girl named Jill in my class at the Annoyance Theater. After one of our classes she had asked me out on a date, and we had been on several dates since then. During the holidays she was going home to her parents, and I wouldn't see her for three weeks. She taught at a private school and had an extended break.

I had called her a few times during the holidays but hadn't been able to get hold of her. The fourth week of separation came and went. Her roommate told me that she had come home but had immediately left and flown to L.A. She had finally called me a couple of days earlier, and we had met for dinner the night before I was to meet with Del.

Del was taking way too long. It was a cloudy, snowy day, and I could see his figure through the bank windows. He was talking to someone in line and couldn't see that a teller's window had opened for him. I was sitting in an illegally parked car fifty feet away, but I could see it.

I honked my horn at Del and pointed at the open window. He looked at me and shook his head to let me know that he didn't understand. I pointed again as the woman at the window waved her hand. Del never saw her because he was trying to figure out why I was honking.

Unbelievably, Del got out of line and walked outside to the car. I thought my eyes were going to bounce out of my head.

"What?" Del asked as he slowly walked up to the car window.

"The window all the way down on the end was open," I exclaimed.

"Where?"

"The woman with the red sweater," I said, exasperated.

He threw his hands up in disgust. "I very well can't get to her out here."

"I didn't call you out here," I yelled back.

He started walking back to the bank. "You made me lose my place in line, you twit."

"Can you please pay attention in there?" I called after him.

He opened the door of the bank and bellowed back, "How about you just calm the fuck down. Please."

The customers and employees of the bank bristled as Del walked back in. I imagined that First American Bank hated our weekly visits.

After the bank we went to Roosevelt and Jefferson streets to the UPS building. Del went in to get a package while I remained in the car and fumed over my dinner with Jill.

She and I had filled each other in on our various Christmas activities, and any anxiety I had felt over not speaking for a month had subsided. As dessert arrived, I reached across the table and placed my hand over her left hand and held it for a few minutes.

It took me a few seconds to figure out what the prickly coldness was that was piercing the middle of my palm. I looked at Jill; she was watching me look at my hand. She looked me in the eye for a moment and then looked away because she knew I was going to look at her hand next.

I don't know why I hadn't seen it before, but there it was. A gold band with a diamond rock nestled on top of it.

Del crawled back into the car with a large, thin, square box tucked under his arm. I asked him what was in the box, and he looked at me with a goofy smile. His glasses had fogged up, so it was surreal seeing him facing me with that gigantic, untrimmed grey and white beard framing his large mouth. He was all smiles and no eyes. He looked like a cartoon.

When Del and I got back to his apartment, I carried his things up the stairs. He swung the door open. It was like I was entering a whole new world.

It wasn't immaculate, but it was a miraculous improvement.

Del told me that Charna had sent her cleaning lady over to clean the place up. He stared at me and waited for me to comment.

The only thing I could muster was, "That poor cleaning lady."

Del took off his beret and tossed it on the table. "You are a bowl of fucking jolly today, I'll tell you that."

He sat down and opened his package from UPS. Styrofoam peanuts spilled out onto the floor. I grabbed a broom and tried to contain the mess. Inside the box was a painting. He pulled it out to look at it.

"Look at this. Look at this," he whispered turning it around so I could see it.

It was a picture of a clown holding a balloon.

I smiled and nodded. "It's cute."

Del was beaming. "It's not fucking cute. It's sick. It's twisted. It's beautiful."

I stared at it for a while trying to figure out why it was so demented. It was a simple painting of a clown holding three balloons.

I don't know why I hadn't seen it before, but there it was. In the bottom corner the painting had been signed "J. W. Gacy."

Del just stood there smiling from ear to ear, holding the painting like a lunatic.

"Del," I started, "did you buy a John Wayne Gacy painting?"

He nodded and chuckled with glee. "I'm putting it in the shitter."

He shoved a hammer into my hands, and we marched into the bathroom.

"You're really pouching this moment for me," Del growled. "Cheer up or get out."

I started hammering a nail into the wall. "I'm sorry I'm not sufficiently excited for your serial killer painting."

"He didn't just kill them," Del answered as his voice picked up speed and energy, "he stuffed their underwear down their throats, than raped them, then he killed them."

He was mystified that I wasn't more excited about the fact that he had this painting from the "Killer Clown."

I looked at Del and reached for the painting. He yanked it away from me. "Spit it out. What's the matter with you?" he prodded.

I told him about Jill and how over the Christmas holiday she had gone to a wedding and had met a friend of the groom's father, and they had hit it off. He was eighteen years older than she was, and he was very wealthy. He had his own airplane and had flown her to Shreveport, Louisiana, to watch Notre Dame play in the Independence Bowl. After the game, they flew to Las Vegas and got married.

She and I had only been dating, but it seemed like we were on the verge of becoming a couple. I liked her.

I looked at Del and could see that he was trying to put together something to make me feel better.

"What you should do," he said, "is picture her giving this guy head."

I looked at him and knew he was being very sincere. He really thought this was the answer to my troubles. Atticus Finch, he was not.

I took the picture and hung it on the wall. I looked at Del over my shoulder and said, "The last thing I'm going to do is take relationship advice from someone who's forcing me to hang a self-portrait of a child-molester-slash-serial killer over his toilet."

Just the thought of that made us both laugh.

I went to the kitchen and grabbed my keys while Del took a "trial piss" to see what it would be like to go to the bathroom in front of Pogo the Clown. Unfortunately he didn't shut the door, so we both got the full effect of the experiment.

I started toward the door as Del settled into his chair and flipped on the TV. "What's your rush?" he asked, searching around looking for "X-Files" reruns. "It's not like you've got a girlfriend to go home to."

He was right. He was a jerk but correct nonetheless. He found the channel he was searching for and stood up and poured two cups of hot water. He reached into the cabinet and opened two brand-new tea bags.

I sat down and dipped the tea bag into the water. We sat there for the next three hours and watched WWF wrestling.

11

A Gift from Scruthers

I arrived at Del's apartment a week later to see that the place had returned to its normal state of filth.

Kind of.

The living room and the front side rooms were immaculate, but the kitchen, bedroom, and bathroom were pigsties. He never went into the front rooms, so they just gathered dust.

To my horror, a new smell had been introduced to the apartment. It had actually made me gag a little bit as I walked in. I asked Del what he thought the smell was.

He told me that the cat had escaped to the basement a couple days earlier and had carried something up to the top of the cabinets when it came back.

"You want to climb up there and see what's up there?" Del asked.

No. I did not. Absolutely did not want to see what was up there.

He carried a chair over beside the cabinet, and I stepped up on it anyway. As I reached up, Scruthers jumped down. I followed pretty quickly after him.

I reached the floor and cupped my hand over my mouth. "He's got half a mouse up there." I really thought I was going to throw up.

I ran into the living room and opened a window so that I could breathe some fresh air. What I didn't see was that Del had grabbed a broom and was sweeping it along the top of the cabinet.

Dust flew everywhere. I turned to see him make a second swipe and watched the half-eaten mouse come hurtling toward me.

I yelled and jumped out of the way as the carcass bounced against the wall and landed on the floor. Scruthers pounced on the mouse and ran away with it.

I looked up at Del as he stood in the middle of the kitchen holding the broom.

"Ready to go?" he asked.

Oh yes. I wanted out of there.

Outside, Del stopped at the curb. "Ohh. This is my favorite one yet," Del said, admiring our latest mode of transportation.

It was a beat-up 1976 Ford Ranger pickup truck. Eight hundred dollars' worth of blue, dented steel. Up to that point I had been borrowing cars to drive Del around. My dad had found the truck in a parking lot in Sullivan, Illinois, with a "For Sale" sign on it. I sent him the money and he drove it up to me. Del loved it.

He crawled in and bounced up and down on the long bench seat. We took our initial voyage in the pickup and pointed it in a familiar direction.

As we slipped into a booth at the Golden Nugget, the waitress frowned and walked away. It was probably the smell.

She brought our drinks, and Del ordered for the both of us. I knew what was coming as soon as he asked me what I was getting.

"I'll have the horseshoe, and my little retarded friend will have the Kansas City omelet," he said as she wrote down our order.

She departed and Del kicked me under the table. "Let's talk," he growled.

"You don't have to kick me to talk to you. I'm sitting right here," I snapped at him.

"I wanted to get your attention," he said.

It really wasn't that big of a deal, but it annoyed me that he had kicked me. "I'm staring right at you. I'm not sure how you can get any more of my attention."

"Will you just pipe down and listen to me," he barked.

I rubbed my leg under the table. So far he had kicked me in the shin and launched a partially eaten mouse at me.

"Are you happy?" he asked me.

I didn't know where he was going with his inquisition, but I answered, "I guess. Sure, I'm happy."

"If you're so goddamn happy, why do you insist on always playing angry, arguing assholes on stage?"

He had caught me off guard. I didn't know how to answer.

"Maybe you're funny and maybe you get some laughs, but you're a bully and a stage hog, and the rest of your classmates are becoming scared of you."

I sat there, taking my whipping. I had learned at a young age that I was never to argue with a director or teacher. It was a humbling experience to have my flaws pointed out, but I wasn't much of an actor or student if I couldn't withstand the criticism.

"And I'm tired of you arguing in every fucking scene in class. That's something new that you started doing, and I want it to stop."

I looked for the waitress and prayed for my food to arrive. I was listening and accepting my scolding. I just wanted something to fidget with while he was doing it.

"People work at jobs they hate. Are married to people they don't like. Have children they wish they never had. Why do you think they want to go to an improv club and watch you fight and argue more than they do? They're coming here for an escape, not to be reminded how fucked up and miserable they are."

My napkin was now in shreds. Del's glasses were at the end of his nose. He looked at me over the top of his rims.

"I'm not saying you can never argue. But you're stronger if you don't. Arguing is the lazy improviser's way of dealing with an issue. You're better than that."

Our food arrived, but neither of us ate it. I used the fork to push it around and listened to what he wanted me to hear.

"Did you want to defend yourself?" he asked as he wound down.

"Nope," I answered.

"Did you want to comment on what I said?" he prodded again.

"You won't have to tell me again," I said, taking a bite of the omelet. "I'll do better."

"Good," he said, trying to wipe the cheese out of his beard.

Things returned to normal. We talked about "X-Files" and how he wanted to buy a laser pointer so he could play with the cat.

We finished our meal and ran the rest of our errands. As we left the grocery store, Del paused at the entrance and dug around in the ashtray for cigarette butts.

He rummaged through the sand and ashes until he found three or four that were long enough for him to smoke. He deposited them in his green army jacket and walked back to the car.

I dropped him off and headed home. I showered as soon as I got home and prepared to go to IO to watch some shows. My roommate Mike was also taking classes and was in my group, Monkey Rocket. He decided he would go with me, and we crawled into my truck.

"It smells horrible in here," Mike said as he shut the door.

I closed my eyes and inhaled. He was right. My new eight-hundred-dollar truck smelled like Del.

12

A Trim

I didn't even recognize Del the next time I saw him. He was outside waiting for me, and I had walked right by him and started toward the gate that led to his apartment.

"Hey, nitwit. I'm right here," he hollered at me as I tried to ring his bell.

His long, scraggly, mangy beard had been trimmed and cleaned to a short, sharp cut. His hair had been washed and cut, and he was wearing a long-sleeve black knit shirt.

"Oh my God," I said in wonder as I looked him over. "What happened to you?"

"I had to go get new head shots this morning," he said almost embarrassingly.

As we drove, I kept turning and looking at him. Eventually he got annoyed and yelled at me to stop looking at him.

"I can't help it. You look like a completely different person. You're really going to scare the crap out of your students," I told him.

"Why do you say that?" he asked me. "Do you think my students are scared of me?"

"They're pretty intimidated. Now with your new look, you look like a Harvard professor," I told him.

To my surprise, that hurt his feelings. "I don't want to scare or intimidate anybody. I want respect, not fear. Fear never taught anything." He said all of this very quietly and then added, "Remind me never to trim my beard again. I'd rather look like a homeless kook then a pretentious prick at some university."

13

Ghosts

Tourism in Chicago falls off quite a bit in the winter months, so I took a job as a host at Second City. It didn't pay much, but it was pretty simple and allowed me to make a little extra money to live on.

The job required me to take people to their seats and to monitor the crowds during the show. Once the show was over, the hosts were in charge of putting the chairs on the tables and picking up the garbage that was lying around the theater. We helped bus the tables for the waitresses and tried to get the room ready for the cleaning crew.

The greatest benefit of hosting at Second City was that I was able to sit in a chair off to the side of the audience and watch the greatest performers in the city amuse and amaze a room filled with appreciative audiences. At the time I was working at Second City, the main stage cast consisted of Stephnie Weir, Rachel Dratch, Kevin Dorf, Rich Tellarico, Jim Zulevic, and Rachel Hamilton. Jeff Richmond was directing the cast as they worked at writing and improvising a new show. I was lucky enough to witness the process of putting a revue together from beginning to end.

Del came to watch the show at Second City one evening and decided to wait for me to finish so that I could give him a ride home. He sat in a chair by the rail while I walked around helping clean up the theater. All the performers, directors, and producers stopped by to speak with him. They were all very gracious, and Del seemed to enjoy the attention.

Once I finished my duties, I grabbed my coat from the kitchen and walked out to see Del. There were a few people milling about, but it was pretty empty and most of the lights were off. I asked Del if he was ready to leave and he said yes, but he remained seated.

"You all right?" I asked him.

He nodded and took a deep breath as he looked around the room, absorbing the moment. "My, my, my, my. I forgot what it's like in here when it's dark and empty," he said.

"A lot of ghosts in here," I told him.

"Don't I know it," he responded. "The problem is I knew all the ghosts when they were alive," he said, laughing at that revelation.

"You miss it?"

"Sometimes," he answered. "Not often but sometimes. Second City is like the Masons or the Mafia. Once you're a member of it, you're never not a member."

He was introspective for a few moments. "I did my time, you know. We grew away from each other, Second City and I. It's sad, but it was time for the two of us to go our separate ways. I'm not sure who's here or what they do, and that's the way it should be. I took this theater as far as I could take it, and now it's time for this new generation of performers to take it places I could only dream about."

"You could direct a show here tomorrow and it would be great," I told him, and I genuinely believed it.

"Oh, I'm sure it would be. I'm a better director now than I've ever been. But I wouldn't be the same director I am today if I spent the last fifteen years here at Second City. I needed to move away from here to grow and develop.

"Leaving Second City was the best thing that happened to both of us. I needed to leave, and they needed me to be gone. It was the same for Bernie Sahlins and Paul Sills. The cast constantly changed and that was helpful to keep everything fresh, but the theater didn't continue its evolution until all the old guard stepped aside and let the new voices take steps to the next level.

"It's the same way for ImprovOlympic. One day Charna and I will wake up and see that the old way we used to teach is archaic and outdated. It's advancing and developing so rapidly that the only way to allow it to survive and thrive is for Charna and I to step aside and let the new guard lead it past the next threshold.

"I remember when Viola Spolin would come to do workshops with us while I was working here in the early sixties. She would run us through these exercises, and we would stand behind her and roll our eyes. Her style was so outdated and she was so out of touch, and we felt that her old idea of how it all should be done was stifling our creativity. Very soon Charna and I will be in the same position as poor Viola. It will be humbling, but I'll gladly step aside because I'll know that improvisation as an art form has made a giant leap forward. My only fear is that I won't realize I've become antiquated and that I'll be running around looking like an old fool."

Del had been very sentimental lately, and his stories all had a twinge of sadness to them. He had told me often that he was finished with the Second City part of his life, but I could tell that there was still a small part that was incomplete.

"I really loved this place," he said, smiling. "I can look up at that stage and see myself up there running around with Severn and Bill Alton and Zhora Lampert. I had some awful battles here, and there were times that I was a complete shit. But the people draw you back. The Joyce Sloans, the Don Depollos, the Barbara Harrises—those are the people you come back for.

"Look at that stage. You stand on that stage and you stand on the same stage where the legends of comedy have held court. That's the same stage that men and women were anointed as kings and queens. John Belushi, Severn Darden, Bill Murray, Fred Willard, Fred Kaz, Danny Aykroyd, Gilda Radner, Harold Ramis, John Candy, Joe Flaherty, George Wendt, Shelley Long, David Steinberg, Mina Kolb, Alan Myerson, Peter Boyle, John Brent, Avery Schreiber . . ."

Every name that Del mentioned sounded like a bullet out of a gun. He wasn't simply remembering the names, he was firing them at me like a pistol. The list was endless, but every name he spoke had the same importance.

When he had exhausted the list, he sat there quietly biting his lip. I could tell that he didn't really want to leave.

"Do you want me to go back to the kitchen and get you something to drink?" I asked him.

He shook his head and reached for his winter army jacket. "No, we should be leaving. Once again I've overstayed my welcome here."

14

The Golden Dome

We were lost. Del was scheduled to teach a workshop and had drafted me to drive. The class was to take place with a group of artists and was scheduled to begin that evening at eight. I looked at my watch. It was 8:30.

Del kept looking at the sheet of paper where he wrote the address. He squinted out the window, looking for address numbers on houses. It was difficult to see because it was a dark, cloudy evening. The streetlights didn't illuminate much.

"I thought you said this was going to be in a hotel." I was driving very slowly while I squinted out the window.

"That's what they fucking said," he responded.

There were no hotels to be found. This was purely a residential area on the West Side of the city. The rundown abandoned buildings only heightened the tension. We were lost and not exactly in the best area.

"We should ask for directions," I told him.

"From where?" he answered. "I haven't seen a business or gas station since we crossed the Kennedy Expressway!"

He set his sheet of paper on the seat. I looked at it and saw the address, 3737 Washington. There wasn't a chance it was East Washington because the East Side of the city stretched only four blocks. We deduced it had to be on the West Side, but it looked bleak.

He had written down a phone number, but it wasn't going to do us any good because neither of us had a cell phone. If we found a pay phone we could pull over, but it seemed like that would be similar to finding an oasis in the desert.

"I can't recall having seen a vehicle in the last half-hour," Del said.

It was pretty desolate. I turned the truck around and drove down Washington again. Very few of the homes had numbers. The place that looked like it might be 3737 West Washington had only three walls and no roof. It looked as if at one time there had been a second floor, but it now resided permanently in the open area of the ground level.

"I guess 'sit, stand, lean' is out," Del said, referring to an old Viola Spolin short-form game.

We had driven up the same block three times hoping the numbers 3737 would magically appear. We had exhausted all our options in this location.

"Maybe it's 4747 West Washington," I proposed.

"Jesus," Del sighed. "That's going to put us farther into this mess."

"I don't know what else to do, Del. This obviously isn't where you're supposed to be, so I'm just throwing out some other options. Do you have any ideas besides driving into that darkness?"

He scratched his dirty beard and grimaced. "Deep into that darkness peering, long I stood there wondering, fearing, Doubting, dreaming dreams no mortal ever dared to dream before; But the silence was unbroken, and the stillness gave no token, And the only word there spoken was the whispered word, 'Lenore?'—This I whispered, and an echo murmured back the word, 'Lenore!' Merely this and nothing more."

"I surmise that to mean you have no ideas."

"Drive on dear boy, and let's see what awaits us," Del answered.

"Well, it won't be a raven," I replied.

He acted surprised that I recognized his poetry reference. "You said 'into that darkness,' and that was the first thing that entered my mind."

"I'm a little surprised you would quote Edgar Allan Poe. I would think you'd find him to be a little too pedestrian and popular."

Del smiled. He recited:

"The crowd was famish'd by degrees; but two of an enor-
    mous city did survive,
And they were enemies: they met beside
The dying embers of an altar-place
Where had been heap'd a mass of holy things
For an unholy usage; they rak'd up,
And shivering scrap'd with their cold skeleton hands
The feeble ashes, and their feeble breath
Blew for a little life, and made a flame
Which was a mockery; then they lifted up
Their eyes as it grew lighter, and beheld
Each other's aspects—saw, and shriek'd, and died—
Even of their mutual hideousness they died,
Unknowing who he was upon whose brow
Famine had written Fiend.
The world was void,
The populous and the powerful was a lump,
Seasonless, herbless, treeless, manless, lifeless
A lump of death—a chaos of hard clay.
The rivers, lakes and ocean all stood still,
And nothing stirr'd within their silent depths;
Ships sailorless lay rotting on the sea,

And their masts fell down piecemeal: as they dropp'd
They slept on the abyss without a surge—
The waves were dead; the tides were in their grave,
The moon, their mistress, had expir'd before;
The winds were wither'd in the stagnant air,
And the clouds perish'd;
Darkness had no need of aid from them—
She was the Universe."

He waited for me to respond. "I don't know that one," I said.

"I didn't think you would. It's Lord Byron," he said. For extra measure he added, "You little fucker."

As we slid west on Washington, the buildings were replaced by trees and lagoons. We went from being intimidated to intrigued. It was amazing to think we were still in Chicago.

"It's the lagoons, Del. We're in Garfield Park." I was relieved I finally knew where we are.

The dome of the administration building, with its golden roof, stood out in the chilly winter evening. Abraham Lincoln was captured in the statue "The Rail Splitter," which stood guarding the sanctity of the beautiful esplanade.

"Do you think your workshop is in the dome?" I asked Del. He shrugged his shoulders, so I pointed us toward the administration building.

I picked up the sheet with the address and phone number and walked toward the entrance. Del stayed in the truck as I tried to figure out where we were supposed to go. The security guards weren't expecting any workshop. They looked at me like I was crazy as I tried to explain improv to them. If there was a workshop at Garfield Park, it was news to them. My watch showed that it was a little past 9:30.

As I returned to the truck, Del was standing beside the truck talking to a menacing figure. I stopped in my tracks, afraid to approach the two of them. The mysterious young man was wearing a hooded winter coat with a baseball cap pulled down low, hiding his face. He kept his hands in his coat pockets, which made me very nervous. I couldn't imagine what he was holding in there.

"I'll give you a gram for sixty dollars," he told Del. I could see that he was missing his front teeth, top and bottom.

"Not interested," Del informed him.

"C'mon. You're not going to get any better than sixty bucks."

"I told you what I wanted," Del said.

"Shit!" yelled the young man. He turned and ran past me into the darkness.

"What was that?" I asked.

"I'm buying some grass," Del cackled with glee. "Do you know how long it's been since I've bought anything from someone on the street?"

I was shocked. I started to object, but the young man reappeared out of the dark, charging toward us. Instinctively I opened the door, pushed Del in the truck, and sped around to the driver's side and clambered in.

I started the engine as he banged on the window and yelled at Del to roll down the window. I started to pull away, but Del opened the door and handed the man a ten-dollar bill. In return he tossed a plastic bag onto Del's lap. In an instant he ran away, disappearing into the night. I slipped the gearshift into drive, heading west on Washington once again.

There were two marijuana cigarettes in the baggie, and Del took them out to inspect them thoroughly. "One for me and one for you," he pronounced.

"I don't want it."

"I guess I'll just have to smoke it for you," he said.

My heart was racing. "I can't believe you did that. That was incredibly dangerous."

"Am I to understand that the dome building wasn't the location of my workshop?" Del asked.

The fear of the moment forced me to forget the workshop momentarily. My mind was still focused on the fact that Del had just bought some pot from a random stranger in a parking lot on the West Side of Chicago.

The trees and lagoons disappeared again as the buildings and homes returned. The neighborhoods seemed even more dilapidated. The businesses we passed were closed for the evening with metal gates locked tightly across the doors. A deserted gas station sat empty as we passed the 4200 block.

4747 West Washington was a bust. Neither of us was surprised to see that it contained nothing more than an empty lot, full of garbage.

The deserted gas station looked as if it had a pay phone hanging on the building as we passed it again on our way back. I pulled in and parked the truck at the gas pump.

As I walked toward the building, I saw Del push the cigarette lighter on the dashboard. I walked back and motioned for him to roll down the window.

"Don't smoke that in my truck," I ordered him.

"You've got to be kidding me," he said, exasperated.

"Not in the truck, Del."

The dashboard lighter popped out and Del lit his joint. "I'm getting out, you whiny prude."

I opened the door for him and turned away. "Firecracker," he yelled, and motioned for me to come back to the truck. He unzipped my jacket and stuffed the plastic bag into my shirt pocket.

"I'm not holding your other joint," I yelled.

"Just trust me, you little pansy," he snapped.

Del mumbled and complained as he got out of the truck while I walked toward the phone. I dialed the number on Del's paper and was eventually connected to the woman who was in charge of the event where Del was supposed to teach.

"It's all over. Don't worry about it now," the woman said to me when I explained to her what had happened.

"Where was it?" I asked her.

"Gallery 37. The old Block 37 on Washington Street," she answered. I closed my eyes and grimaced. I understood why Del was confused. In the Chicago grid system, Block 37 was located at Washington and State. It had attracted quite a bit of publicity of late because it was an empty block right in the middle of the Loop. It was a bit of an embarrassment for Mayor Daley and the city that such a prime spot of real estate would sit dormant for so many years. Newspapers and media began calling the area by its official name, which according to the grid was Block 37. A summer institute for art students occupied the empty area during the school break. The program was called Gallery 37.

Del had heard Gallery 37 on Block 37 at Washington Street. The woman realized that she probably should have worded it differently and apologized for the misunderstanding.

While I talked to the woman about rescheduling, I watched Del in the reflection of the glass of the empty gas station. He was close to finishing his joint as I expressed my regrets once again to the woman on the phone. A blue light flashed in the glass of the window, which caused me to drop the phone and turn around to look at Del. Without his realizing it, a Chicago Police Department squad car had pulled up and parked beside the truck.

My throat tightened as I tried to holler out to Del. All I could manage was a squeak, but it got the point across. He puffed on his joint as he turned and looked at the officers who stepped out of the police vehicle.

"This station is closed, gentlemen," the tall cop announced.

"I know," I squawked. "We were just using the phone."

Del smoked the last of his joint and then, without extinguishing it, swallowed the entire thing. While it was shocking, it was one of the luxuries of being a former fire-eater.

The two officers stopped in their tracks. "Did you just eat your cigarette?" asked the blonde cop.

"Buzz off, turkey," growled Del.

The officers became agitated at Del's response as they sauntered over to inspect him more closely. His demeanor remained the same as they asked him more questions and started patting him down.

The tall officer walked over to me as I tried to explain the situation. "I'm sorry about the way my friend is acting. He was supposed to teach a class tonight and there was a huge mix-up, so he's a little upset."

He aimed his flashlight at my eyes. "He a relative of yours?"

"No," I explained. "He's my teacher."

"Well, your teacher was smoking what appeared to us to be an illegal substance. Would you know anything about that?" he asked me.

"That kid has never touched anything illegal in his entire life," Del shouted at the officer closest to me. "Why don't you pigs come and hassle me. I'm the lawbreaking senior citizen. I'm the demographic that poses the most threat to you assholes, aren't I? Thank God the two of you took a break from stopping all those gangbangers, rapists, and murderers so that you could harass an old man and his little retarded friend."

As Del taunted and angered the officers, my mind focused on one thought: the baggie in my shirt pocket. The officer stepped forward, and I stepped back and gasped. My shocked reaction surprised him, causing him to flinch.

"Listen, as long as you're clean, we're going to leave the two of you alone. Tell your friend to shut up," he reassured me. He instructed me to turn around and put my hands on the building as he patted me down. He checked me over to make sure I wasn't carrying anything dangerous. He patted a little too hard on my groin and caused me to recoil. The cop had just racked me.

"Sorry about that," he apologized. He put his hands in my pants pockets and pulled out money along with various credit cards. As I felt him unzip my coat jacket, my heart started racing. It was beating so fast and hard I was sure he could hear it. His hand reached up to my shirt pocket and my mind went blank. Everything around me grew fuzzy and seemed to move in slow motion. It seemed impossible to keep my eyes open. The officer pulled the baggie out of my pocket and inspected it.

Del was mouthing off to the other police officer and wasn't paying attention to what was happening with me. In my sudden state of panic, one thought raced through my head: "I should make a run for it."

"Run for what?" asked the officer.

To my horror, my inner thoughts had managed to escape my lips. My mind had betrayed me and allowed me to say aloud what I was only thinking.

"What did you have in this?" the officer asked as he shook the baggie in my face. It was empty.

"Cards," Del yelled at him. "He had his playing cards in that bag."

The officer left me standing against the wall and walked back to Del. I continued standing against the wall because I was afraid if I moved away from it, I would collapse to the ground. The two cops proceeded to rummage through the truck and found nothing but a deck of cards I kept in the glove compartment.

"How are you doing?" Del asked as I walked back to the truck.

"Shut up." My legs were still a bit rubbery, but I could walk on them again. The officers finished inspecting the truck and instructed us to get back inside, but not to turn on the engine.

"Where is it? Where's the second joint?" I asked Del once we were inside the truck and out of their earshot.

"I ate it."

"When?" I asked.

"Right when I saw the lights. I ate the second one and swallowed the weed I was smoking."

"Why did you put the baggie in my pocket?" I asked.

"I didn't want to carry it around. And I wanted to see if you would trust me," he answered.

"I almost had a heart attack, you old idiot!" I yelled. He broke into hysterical laughter. I couldn't tell if it was because he thought I was funny or because the marijuana had begun to take effect.

The officer returned and gave me a ticket for having an expired registration. He told me I could get the registration renewed within thirty days and wouldn't have to pay a fine. I thanked him as I rolled up the window.

Del rolled down the window and yelled, "See you later, Officer McCronkey," as we pulled back onto Washington. They followed us all the way downtown to make sure we didn't make any stops along the way.

We drove by Block 37, and I pointed it out to Del as I explained what had happened. It didn't matter. He was way too high to understand.

15

Back to New York

When the Compass Players closed in St. Louis, Del went east and tried to settle back into the New York scene. Elaine May and Mike Nichols ventured to New York too, but a performance trio was not in the works. Nichols and May signed a contract with a talent agency and became an enormously successful and high-profile comedy duo. They were booked in theaters and on television shows around the country.

Del kept in touch with Elaine, but their romance had begun to unravel. She was too busy to sustain a serious relationship.

Now Del began doing stand-up comedy in clubs around the city. The pressure of supporting himself by telling jokes pushed him to address personal issues he'd previously ignored. Sometimes he wouldn't leave his apartment for weeks at a time. Once he went a week barely eating or sleeping as he contemplated his father's suicide.

His friends began to think he'd gone crazy and encouraged him to get professional help. He was twenty-two years old, and he too questioned his sanity. He got financial aid to receive therapy from Sigmund Freud's prize pupil, Theodor Reik.

"The repressed memory is like a noisy intruder being thrown out of the concert hall. You can throw him out, but he will bang on the door and continue to disturb the concert. The analyst opens the door and says, 'If you promise to behave yourself, you can come back in.'" Del often recited this quote from Reik. His other favorite was, "Work and love—these are the basics. Without them, there is neurosis."

He was never cured, but he became well enough to function in society. Somewhat.

His percussion skills earned him a little money: he took small jobs playing drums for television specials. He was the fire-eating drummer in the NBC presentation of "Aladdin" and a Salvation Army major who played the bass drum in "Gift of the Magi."

Comedy clubs weren't paying enough, so Del borrowed money from Elaine and took jobs as a typist at a few places. Severn Darden told Del he could make extra money by participating in medical research at local institutions. So Del enrolled in an REM sleep program run by the air force. He would travel to Brooklyn to sleep and allow them to measure his brain activity, all for the Mercury 12 space program.

At these sessions Del was first introduced to LSD. Part of the air force research demanded that Del take acid under observation, presumably to determine who dealt better with being cooped up in a tiny space capsule, an extrovert or an introvert. Del was, of course, the extroverted side of the test.

In one instance he popped a tab and was placed in an isolation capsule. After the LSD kicked in, Del found himself flying through the cosmos. Several hours into the trip, he reported, the hatch opened and a shaft of bright light shined in accompanied by a white-gloved hand. The hand held a sheet of paper in front of Del's face while a booming voice echoed in his ears. In his altered state, Del thought he had died and was meeting God.

"What do you want for lunch?" rang down from the heavens.

Del scanned the sheet of paper, amused by the delicacies served in the sweet hereafter. The hatch slammed shut, sending Del rocketing through the galaxy once again. An hour later the hatch opened and the white-gloved hand reached into the pod to deliver a tuna salad sandwich. "Thanks Jesus," Del replied.

After two years of touring the stand-up circuit in New York, Del filled a suitcase with peyote and returned to St. Louis to appear in *The Nervous Set*, the first beat musical that portrayed the real-life antics of some of America's giants: Jack Kerouac, Allen Ginsberg, John Clellon Holmes, and Jay Landesman. Co-written by his old Compass director, Ted Flicker, the show explored the world of the beat generation. It was a huge hit despite its three-hour-and-forty-five-minute running time.

Del had neglected to notify the dream lab in Brooklyn of his St. Louis gig. He soon received a letter that read, "Dear Mr. Close: You still owe the United States Air Force one dream."

When the producers of *The Nervous Set* decided to take the show to New York, Del went along to appear in his first Broadway production. But the show was simply too weird for the Great White Way. Its absence of choreography, its four-piece jazz combo on stage, and its general lack of interest in any of the conventions of the Broadway musical contributed to a quick demise. It closed after twenty-one days.

Back on the stand-up comedy circuit, Del polished his routine to the point where he was making enough money to support himself. He now recorded a comedy album, *The Do-It-Yourself Psychoanalysis Kit*, inspired by his therapy sessions. Elaine May helped Del organize and write some of the material.

The album sold moderately well and enabled Del to do his stand-up routine in clubs that were frequented by high-profile comedians. He wasn't considered to be an A-list talent, but he had risen to being an opening act for Lenny Bruce, Mort Sahl, and Shelley Berman.

After Del was arrested for smoking marijuana in an alley in New York, he was denied a cabaret card to do stand-up in the city. He crossed the country to California and began performing his routine to enlightened audiences on the West Coast. Del admired Lenny Bruce, and his act was heavily influenced by Bruce's work. The two of them were friends who spent a great deal of time discussing art, literature, and their distrust of government. They both felt they had a social responsibility to educate an audience instead of simply entertaining it. And Del supplied Lenny with speed whenever he needed it.

In Hollywood at the Club Resistance in 1960, Del had a phone call from his former Compass Players cast mates in Chicago. Six months earlier they had formed a new group they called The Second City, and had been well received by Chicago audiences. The group had some internal problems and wanted Del to come and help direct the company. Paul Sills was the primary director, but Bernie Sahlins and Howard Alk believed that Del could be brought in to balance the relationship between director and cast.

In short order, Del was on his way to Chicago. He would leave for a few brief stints, but it would be his home for the rest of his life.

16

Commit! Commit!

I had a bag of garbage that I had carried down from Del's apartment to dispose of behind his house. When I got back to the truck, someone was leaning inside the passenger's side window.

My initial thought was that Del was being robbed, but as I got closer the stranger seemed too cavalier to be menacing. I stepped up, and Del motioned for me to get in the car so that we could drive away.

He was leaning back away from the window as the man had managed to bend almost the entire top half of his body into the car.

Del stuck out his hand to the man and said, "My little retarded friend is here, so we better get a move on. It was nice to meet you."

The man shook his hand and Del rolled up the window and commanded, "Drive, Firecracker, drive." I waited for Del to tell me who the man was, but he was prattling on about something he had seen on the news.

Once we arrived at the Jewel store on Ashland, I asked Del about the strange man.

"A fan," was all that he would reveal.

"Of what?" I asked with a little too much surprise in my voice.

"Apparently they showed *The Untouchables* on TV last night. He saw me get into the truck and recognized me, so he came up and talked to me."

Del was on his knees in the bread section looking for his precious dense pumpernickel. He broke away from his search to look up at me for my reaction. He was annoyed to see that I was amused by the entire situation.

"You know," he said, "it's not unusual for me to get recognized wherever we go. I'm a bit of a celebrity in this town."

I knew that the next thing I wanted to say would piss him off, and I thought twice about saying it—but fired anyway. "If you're such a celebrity, how come anytime I mention your name, nobody knows who the hell I'm talking about?"

He used the shopping cart to lift himself back up to his feet. He leaned his face within an inch of mine and sneered, "Because the people you spend all your time with are fucking idiots."

He reached down and picked up the bread and slammed it into the cart. A normal loaf of bread would have been smashed by the throw. This bread was so hard I thought it had dented the shopping cart.

He pushed the cart ahead and walked several steps in front of me. He was mad, seething mad.

A couple of times in class I had seen him get angry. The first time was an incident that had occurred in several classes. If someone was doing really poorly and just wasn't getting it, Del would pull out his checkbook and say, "I'm sorry, we've obviously misled you somewhere in your training here. You've managed to advance through five levels of classes without learning a single goddamn thing about improvisation."

He would then write out a refund check, and the person would disappear. That happened to a fellow student in my class. Del had added as she walked away, "Take a cooking class or something, but I'd encourage you to stay away from the stage."

In the second incident he had told a female student that her mugging and posturing in scenes were so awful that he encouraged her to sew her vagina shut so that she didn't produce any offspring who might have her despicable talents.

He was also angry with her because she was constantly yawning in his class. That drove him nuts.

To Del's credit, she *was* really bad. Not necessarily "vagina sewing" bad, but pretty awful.

I had heard that Del could be abusive in class, but there were only those few isolated incidents when I saw it happen. The rest of the time he was informative, constructive, and eloquent. But when he snapped, you pulled up a seat and watched the massacre.

As we walked through the aisles of the store, I knew he was furious with me. He tossed a couple of gallons of grape juice into the cart and turned to me and growled, "You know, your constant barrage of bullshit is awfully tiresome."

I bit my lip to keep from smiling.

He was still fuming as we stood in line to check out. He was so mad that he didn't realize the person in front of us had already gone through the line. The cashier was motioning for us to move through. She finally got Del's attention, and we moved forward.

Del pulled out his wallet and started to apologize. "I'm sorry," he said, "my little re—"

Before he could utter the words "my little retarded friend," I interrupted him and said, "My Grandpa drifts off sometimes.

We need to get him home so he gets his nap in. I'm sorry you had to wait for us."

At the mention of the word "Grandpa," Del's head twisted around so fast that I thought it had snapped off his neck.

"Grandpa" had trumped "little retarded friend."

Del started to tell the woman that he wasn't my grandfather, but he thought better of it and tossed his money down in front of her. He walked out of the store and straight to the truck. I collected his change from the cashier and wheeled his groceries out to the truck. I loaded everything into the flatbed and headed back to his home.

He was silent the entire trip. I asked him questions and talked to him, but he refused to respond. As soon as I pulled up in front of his apartment, he crawled out of the truck and slammed the door. He walked straight upstairs and left me there to bring everything up.

Once everything was unpacked, I told him I was leaving, but he stared straight ahead watching his TV.

The next night I was at ImprovOlympic when an intern came and told me that I had a phone call. It was Del.

"Send an intern over to 4211 North Wolcott. A student of mine just taped something that I want you to see," he boomed at me through the phone.

Several hours later I arrived home and popped in the tape. It was the "Dennis Miller Live" show on HBO. Right in the middle of the interview with Jon Lovitz, a former "Saturday Night Live" actor, Miller had said, ". . . and you've got Del Close in the background yelling, 'Commit! Commit!'"

I replayed it a couple of times to make sure I had heard it right.

"That was pretty cool," I told Del when I called him the next day.

"Yes, it was," he responded. "And the next time your fucking idiot friends ask you who I am, you can show them that tape."

His celebrity status was no longer in question, and he was happy.

17

Sunlamps and Old Men

It was surprisingly warm for a late January afternoon. El Niño was in full effect: it was forty-one degrees.

I was wearing a flannel shirt without a coat. Del had on his beret, two long-sleeve shirts, and no jacket.

Instead of snow, we had a cloud cover that rested over the city, making the days almost as dark as the nights. In this new year we had yet to see the sun. A mist seemed to be constantly present in the air.

Just before we left his apartment, Del and I watched the end of the afternoon news. WGN-TV ran a story about the retail store Sharper Image selling sunlamps at a record pace. The lack of sun was causing people to have bouts with depression. The reporter informed everyone that the sunlamps served as a valuable substitute for the energy and brightness normally supplied by the sun.

I thought it was less of a news story and more of an advertisement for Sharper Image. Del disagreed. "I'm always two steps away from trying to commit suicide again. Without the sun shining, I've got to take an extra step just to see how close to the edge I actually am."

The fact that he said "again" startled me. I didn't know he had ever tried to kill himself. I wasn't sure if he was joking or not, so I asked him if he had seriously tried to knock himself off.

"Oh. Lots of times," he said as a simple matter of fact. "I haven't tried it in a while, though."

It was quiet for a little while, and I could feel my stomach churning. Then he added, "You have no idea how depressing it is to wake up and have it be so goddamn bleak out."

Later, walking out of the grocery store, we saw a confused older couple trying to find their car. They wandered around the parking lot, and Del watched them as I loaded the groceries into the truck. I hadn't been paying attention to them, but Del pointed them out again when I crawled into the truck.

"Do you want me to go help them?" I asked when he told me that he didn't want to leave until they found their car.

"No," he shook his head. "Let's just sit here and see how long it takes them to find it."

We watched for a while; it was clear they were panicking. The woman thought she had found the car and tried to put the key in the lock. Del chortled with glee as she stomped away, unable to get the door open.

"The thing is," Del started, "they're both probably looking for two separate damn cars. He's looking for a Ford they had in '77, and she's looking for a car they drove on vacation in Palm Springs."

As we drove away the old woman was yelling at the old man. Del looked at me and shook his head. "If I ever get like that, I beg you, put me out of my misery. Shoot Charna."

We drove with the window cracked a bit. We were being ridiculous. It really wasn't that warm outside, but it felt downright balmy.

Even with the constant mist, Chicago had yet to record any precipitation for the year. It was a weird winter.

Del visited a particular bookstore weekly and wanted to stop there before we went back to his apartment. They allowed him to trade his books for credit. He snatched up a stack of them and walked into the book hole.

I got out and stood by the truck in front of the store. All of Del's groceries were in the flatbed of the truck, so I had to stay nearby to guard the food.

I had come up with a new plan of action. If we went to get the groceries first, I would have to stay in the truck to guard everything because it was all out there in the open. I increased the urgency by convincing him to buy frozen vegetables and ice cream.

As he exited the truck, I reminded him that he couldn't stay in the store too long because everything would melt. He realized I was right, and he actually hurried inside. I had successfully cut these book-shack visits from three hours to ten minutes.

I could have sat in the truck, but standing beside it reminded Del that I was patrolling his food and prompted him to pick up his pace. I also wanted to stand outside just because it felt so warm.

I leaned against the truck and watched Del inside. He was rummaging around looking for something to buy. He wanted to get something, but he could feel the pressure of my stare. He disappeared into an aisle that was out of my view. I knew he would be there for a while because he wouldn't feel rushed once he was away from my gaze.

Suddenly I became aware of a presence beside me. I ignored it briefly in hopes it would leave me alone, but I saw I would have to acknowledge it or it wouldn't go away.

I turned and was surprised at what I saw.

Standing beside me was an impeccably groomed old man with gleaming, short, silver hair. It was tightly combed and plastered stiffly to his head. He was around my height and a little chubby. The black suit he was wearing was beautiful—probably purchased twenty years earlier but well cared for. His white shirt was starched and tight around his neck, where the folds of his baggy skin settled over his collar. He had on an overcoat and held a fedora hat in his hand as he stood there staring at me.

I asked him if he was okay, and he just kept staring. After a few seconds I could see that there were tears on his face. I couldn't tell if they were there because the wind had caused them or if he had been crying.

Del walked out of the bookstore and stood beside me. "What's this?" he asked, looking suspiciously at the two of us.

As I turned to say I had no idea, the old man finally spoke.

"Sir?" he said to me as his raspy voice cracked. "Can you help me?"

I felt the churning in my stomach again. This whole thing was making me uneasy.

"What do you need help with?" I was trying to be calming as I talked to him, but I realized that I sounded like I was talking to a child.

The old man took a very deep breath. It seemed as though it was hard for him to talk. He was trying to keep his composure as he spoke. After a few deep breaths, he finally managed to say, "I'm lost. I don't know where I am."

I looked at Del. There was a solemn, almost grave look on his face.

"Where are you going?" I asked the old man.

He reached into his pocket and pulled out a small piece of paper. On it was written an address in Evanston.

"I think I got on the wrong train. I was supposed to visit my mother at ten o'clock, but I was confused and nothing looked familiar, so I've been traveling on the train all day," he said, speaking every syllable very slowly.

I looked at my watch. It was almost four. He'd been lost for at least six hours.

While I was worried about the fact that he had been lost for so long, Del had focused on another fact the old man had mentioned.

"Your mother?" Del asked. "How old is your mother?"

"Ninety-eight," the man answered. "She's in a retirement home where we used to live." It was excruciating how long it took him to talk. I hung on every word because I was afraid the next word would be the last I would hear.

Del was amazed this man's mother was still alive. "Jesus," he responded. "How old are you?"

"Eighty-two," he answered.

Del reached his arm out and leaned against the parking meter he was standing beside. He took his hat off and twisted it in his hands. He chewed on his tongue as I looked to get some support from him. He wouldn't make eye contact with me.

"All right," I said, "here's what we're going to do. This is my friend Del. He lives seven blocks from here, but he can't walk there. I want you to stand right here while I take him to his house. It will take me three minutes to get him there and come back. When I get back, I'll drive you to your mother's home."

The man grabbed my hand and began shaking it. His face opened up with relief as he spoke just a little faster. "Thank you, sir. Thank you, sir." He just kept repeating.

Del moved to get in the car, and the old man grabbed Del and hugged him in the middle of the sidewalk. Del patted the man on the shoulder and pulled himself into the cab of the truck.

We sped home and Del hurried out of the truck. I grabbed the groceries; Del snatched up the frozen items.

"Don't worry about these," he shouted. "Hurry up and get back to the old fucker and take him to see his mom."

I saw the concern on Del's face and headed back to the corner of Belmont and Sheffield where we had left the old man.

My stomach dropped as I got closer to the bookstore. He wasn't there.

I got out of the truck and ran into the store to see if anyone knew where he went. No one did.

I ran up and down the street. Down the alley. Into stores. I ran everywhere.

He was gone.

I was still holding the piece of paper that he had handed me with his mother's address on it.

I walked back to the truck with my legs shaking. I started to drive away, but I couldn't gain my composure. I sat in the truck taking deep breaths. I could feel my pulse beating in my arm.

I drove around for a while, but after an hour I went back to Del's and carried his groceries upstairs.

He was watching TV and anxiously turned as I walked in. "Did you get him home to see his mommy?" he joked.

As soon as he saw my face, he realized I hadn't.

"He was gone."

"Jesus," was all he could say.

I deposited his groceries on the table and said goodbye and left.

I drove around the area again looking for the old man, but it was very dark and I soon gave up.

The phone was ringing as I got home. "I tell you I'm depressed and suicidal, and you go ahead and make it worse by killing an old man who has Alzheimer's," Del barked.

I laughed.

We talked for a little while. Del promised not to kill himself if I would go to Sharper Image and buy him a sunlamp. He'd also read that blueberries lower the chances of Alzheimer's. After our experience that day, he wanted me to stop at the store and get him a couple of pints.

"I'm sure the old guy's fine," I said.

Del disagreed. In his mind, he said, I had killed that old man. He was scared that he would be next.

I was glad he had called. He had made me laugh, and I felt better.

I realized that he hadn't called to cheer me up. He had called because he was scared.

He didn't want to die lost and alone.

18

Card Tricks

"Which one of those girls from class is your girl-friend?" Del asked as we walked through the aisles of the Best Buy on North Avenue.

I informed him that I wasn't dating any of them. I was very much single at the time.

"Why don't you date the Big Blonde Girl," he asked. "She's sexy as hell."

And then, as an afterthought, he added, "If my dick could still get hard, she'd be the one that would do it."

I looked around to see if anyone had heard him. Of course, everyone around us had.

"I'm sure she would be ecstatic to hear that," I told him as we walked around looking at VCRs.

"I actually haven't had a solid erection for almost ten years," he mercilessly continued, "but if it was going to happen, she'd be the one to do it."

"Seriously," I pleaded to Del.

His impotence had been a popular topic lately.

A few weeks earlier I had discussed with him how I had recently discovered that there were so many different degrees of status in an improv scene. I had been taught by an instructor that there was high status and low status, but it really wasn't that elementary.

The instructor had given us a deck of cards and told us to draw from the deck to determine our status for the scene. If we drew a seven or above, we were high status. Anything lower was low status.

I had explained to Del that it really shouldn't have been that simple. There were degrees of status. It's not that clear-cut in real life, so it shouldn't be that way in improv. A five of clubs has a different status than a six of hearts, and it should be played that way. Del agreed.

"It's like my dick," he added, "it's not going to get hard, but it's not always completely flaccid. There are degrees of its hardness and softness. It's never going to be the king of hearts again, but every once in a while I can achieve a ten of spades."

To my horror, the following week Del had used that example in his class. He had actually begun the class by saying, "Mr. Griggs and I had an interesting discussion about degrees of status in improv and how it relates to my penis. . . ."

The patrons of Best Buy were now privy to Del's erectile dysfunction. "Why don't you ask the Big Blonde Girl out?" Del asked as I selected a VCR and headed to the checkout counter.

"She's with Eric," I answered.

Del was stunned. "I thought Eric was gay."

I laughed. "You think everybody's gay. He's not gay, he's with the Big Blonde Girl."

Del paid for the VCR. We headed out the door and walked toward Whole Foods. I stopped and put the VCR in the truck. I returned to find Del still contemplating his misjudgment of his student's sexual orientation.

"If Eric's with the Big Blonde Girl, who's Ike with?" Del asked as we walked into the trendy grocery store. "I was sure Eric was boyfriends with Ike."

"Del," I said with a little exasperation, "Ike's not gay either. He has a girlfriend too."

He was befuddled. "I've had this all wrong," he muttered as we wandered through the aisles.

"That's because you operate under two constant misconceptions," I said as we stopped in the vitamin aisle. "Not every guy in your class is gay, and not all your female students are attracted to you."

"Fuck you," he growled. He smiled and added, "They just know I can't do anything about it, so they pursue other options."

"You talking about the guys or the girls?" I asked, biting my lip so I wouldn't grin.

He was silent and stared intensely at the labels on the vitamins.

"Just can't pass up the opportunity to be an asshole, can you?" Del said without shifting his attention away from the shelves of supplements.

I chuckled and walked to the end of the aisle to look for Band-Aids.

He had begun to cough, and it was a particularly ugly flemfest. I walked farther away as he started hacking because I just couldn't handle listening to it. Watching it was no joy either.

His face would contort, and he'd strain his neck forward while his whole body violently lurched in the same direction. It would last for several minutes, always ending with spitting.

It didn't matter where we were. When he was finished, he would hock out whatever had come up, right there on the floor.

I had walked an aisle over and listened for the coughing to subside. I found the Band-Aids and wandered back around. The coughing had stopped, and I could tell it was safe to return. I stared at the floor ahead to make sure I didn't step in whatever Del had spat out.

But the cart was on its side, and Del wasn't where I had left him. I jogged to the end of the aisle and turned the corner. He was face down in the dry goods aisle.

An elderly woman was heading toward me. "He fell down. He fell down," she screeched as she hobbled closer. I stared down at him.

He looked dead.

I was sure he was dead.

The woman was beside me now. "He stumbled forward and bent down, and then he reached out to hold on to the shelf, but he just collapsed."

Del's face was literally nose forward on the ground. Blue boxes of pasta were scattered on the floor. His glasses had fallen on the floor about five feet away from his outstretched right hand, and the frames had broken. The glass had stayed intact, but the left earpiece had snapped off and disappeared under a shelf.

Two employees came running with a manager following close behind. "I think he's drunk," the elderly woman announced.

"He's not drunk," I told her. "He has emphysema." When I bent down to see if he was really dead, Del started coughing. It scared the hell out of me. I didn't want him to be dead, but I wasn't prepared for the fact that he wasn't.

The elderly woman suggested that we turn him over, so the employees tried to roll him onto his back. "I don't think we're supposed to move him," I said as they tried to get a firm grasp on Del's rather large frame.

"That's neck injuries, stupid," the elderly woman snapped.

I gave her a dirty look. There was no reason for her to call me stupid. I didn't know how she came to be in charge of this operation.

Meanwhile Del was regaining consciousness and helped turn himself over. His eyes were wild as he looked around to try to compose himself in his foreign surroundings.

"Jimi Hendrix died on his back," one of the employees piped in. "He threw up and choked to death on his own vomit."

"You don't know what you're talking about," the elderly woman told him. She was talking to the employee, but her statement was intended for me.

Del grabbed the arm of one of the employees and held on to it as he launched into another massive coughing episode.

A dark-haired female employee rushed up and handed Del a bottled water. Her long braided ponytail swung around and smacked Del in the face as she bent down and held the bottle of water to his lips.

She balanced herself by putting her left hand on his knee. This was a perilous moment, but I nonetheless took the time to notice that she was very hot.

When Del finished drinking, he opened his eyes wide and asked the girl, "Is this hell?"

"No," she replied. "It's Whole Foods."

"Same difference," Del responded.

I rolled my eyes. I now had suspicions that he had staged this entire event so he could prattle off that silly little joke.

After a few minutes, they helped Del to his feet. One of the employees left to call an ambulance.

Del put his glasses back on and grabbed my arm. "Let's bolt before they get here and take me away," he said.

The manager of the store trailed behind us yelling that it was store policy that Del had to be taken away in an ambulance. "You'll have to take me away in a straitjacket," Del cackled as he crawled into my truck. I was pretty sure the manager thought the straitjacket might be a good option.

We pulled out of the parking lot and headed back to Del's apartment. I was worried. "Maybe we should have let them take you to the hospital."

"I just lost my balance. I'm okay," he said. He was convincing. He seemed to be okay. He had a red mark on his nose where he had slammed it against the floor.

He looked odd with his earpiece missing from his glasses. I couldn't figure out how they were staying on his face.

"Don't think I'm not keeping track of how many times you've tried to kill me," he said after several moments of silence.

I was wiped out. I had really thought he was dead. "That was scary," I said.

"Was it?"

"Yes," I assured him. "I thought you were dead. It was pretty bad."

"It wasn't all bad," Del said to me. I turned to see he was grinning from ear to ear. "The girl with the ponytail gave me a jack of clubs."

I smiled. "I guess if you're going to go, you might as well go with a jack of clubs."

Del nodded his head, still smiling. "Definitely."

19

Hospitals and Funerals

My grandmother was dying. I had borrowed my room-mate's car and had driven it a few hundred miles to Quincy, Illinois, on a brisk Thursday morning. My mother had called me late Wednesday to tell me that my grandmother's health was failing and most likely this would be the last time I would see her.

I called Del to tell him that I needed to switch days for our errands. I would be picking him up on Friday instead of Thursday. He was irritated, but he reluctantly agreed. I didn't tell him why I needed to switch.

When I got back, I explained to Del why I had been absent. He was fascinated by my journey to see my dying grandmother. He kept asking me to repeat our conversations and listened intently as I described the entire visit.

"Was she in pain?" he asked.

"Excruciating," I answered. "She would take these deep breaths, and you could tell that it was hurting her to breathe." We sat there for a while in his kitchen, contemplating the entire situation.

"Jesus," he exhaled deeply. "I don't want to go out like that. Don't let me die in a hospital."

I looked at Del and could see the sincerity in his face. He stared at death every morning when he looked at the mirror.

I wished I hadn't told him about my grandmother. It had made him a little depressed. I had mentioned it to him in the hope he would console me with some words of wisdom that would put the situation in perspective. Instead Del had begun thinking about his own mortality and had driven me into a deeper saddened state.

I was now in the odd position of trying to console him over my grandmother's impending death.

"Was your grandmother nice?" he asked.

"Sweetest woman I ever met," I answered. "She was very good to me. I feel bad that I didn't make the effort to see her more often."

Del dipped his tea bag in the water and looked toward Scruthers the cat. "If I died today, no one would miss me," he spoke quietly.

His statement surprised me, and I wasn't sure how to answer. I realized that there wasn't a correct answer, I just needed to say something. Anything.

"You're being stupid. Of course you'll be missed," I told him.

He disagreed. "I'll be remembered, but I'd like to be missed."

I started to tell him that I would miss him, but it seemed too awkward to say.

The next morning my phone rang at six. I was lying in bed with my eyes open staring at the ceiling. I knew who it was before I answered it. I picked up the receiver, and my mother informed me that my grandmother had died. I was sad, but there was an amazing feeling of relief that I'd been able to visit her before she passed.

The news hadn't surprised me. She was in too much pain to survive much longer.

When I hung up the phone, it rang again immediately. It was Del.

"I think your grandmother died?" Del said over the phone.

"She did. My mom just called to tell me," I said. I was sad, sleepy, and confused all at once.

"Why are you calling me this early?" I asked him.

"I woke up and had a feeling that something had happened. I thought I'd call you and tell you to call your parents to see if anything had happened."

"That's creepy," I told him.

Del had been initiated as a Wiccan Witch in the late 1980s. The morning my grandmother died, Del had become restless and had felt the passing of a spiritual being into an alternate existence. He had wondered if it was my grandmother and called me.

"I think I'm next," he said. I tried to get him off the phone so I could get back to sleep.

"You always think you're next," I reminded him.

"I'm bound to be right one of these times," he responded.

20

Damaged Goods

We had skipped the last three Thursdays because of bad weather, so Del and I decided to run all our errands after his class on Sunday. When I picked him up at ImprovOlympic, I could tell he was mad as he opened the door.

"Where the hell were you yesterday?" he yelled at me as he pulled himself into the cab of the truck.

I had had to skip the last part of Del's class so that I could go home to central Illinois to watch a play at my old college. Del didn't care.

"Don't miss again," he growled. "Where was your roommate and that hyper chick you're always with?"

They had gone with me. I had actually told Del that the three of us would be missing, but I'd made a mistake when I told him. I had used their names.

Del didn't know names. He knew my name, but that was it. Everyone else was reduced to a physical description. And usually it wasn't a very flattering description.

In my class alone we had:

The Fat Chick

The Asshole

The Little Greek Guy

The Guy That Always Wears the Red Sweat Suit
The Dumb Curly Blonde Bitch
The Tall Blonde Chick
The Anorexic Bald Guy
The Chubby Gay Guy
The Lesbian Lawyer
The Dumb Cunt
The Fat Dumb Cunt
Mr. Clueless
That Useless Son of a Bitch

Sometimes he would call them by their descriptions even though he knew their names. Jason Chin was director of the ImprovOlympic Training Center and had taken Del's class numerous times. Jason talked to Del several times a week and Del knew him well, but Del never referred to him by name. When Del talked about Jason, he always called him The Chinaman.

Apparently The Tall Blonde Chick had missed class as well. Del was not pleased. It was not that the four of us were anything special, but the chemistry of the class was completely thrown.

"The group mind was destroyed. You turned your back on your commitment to them," Del barked at me.

"I had to go, Del. I had to go see the show, and it was my brother Jacob's birthday," I whined back at him.

"You took the whole fucking class with you," he snarled.

My roommate had to go with me, but I had actually talked Jackie, the hyper chick, into skipping class.

"There was a gigantic hole in the group mind, and they couldn't pull it together. Their scene work was bad, the chemistry was off, and they floundered around like they'd never been on stage before." He paused to catch his breath.

He started to gripe at me again but had to stop to cough up a lung. I was happy for the break.

Del regained his composure and spat out the window. I looked in the passenger's side mirror to see if whatever he had spat had landed on the truck. I couldn't tell.

The final straw for the class had been when Mr. Clueless did a scene in which he tried to have sex with a cat.

"He thought it was pretty cute to stand up there and fuck a cat. That in itself I'm not averse to," Del told me. "I've had to sexually satisfy a cat or two while they were in heat, but this twit thought it would be cute to pretend like he was doing it with his dick. A dick won't fit in a cat's asshole. You have to use your pinky finger."

Somehow this bad conversation had turned into a nightmare. Del could see I was horrified.

"That's the most disgusting thing I've ever heard," I groaned at him.

"Sometimes the only thing to calm a cat in heat is to put some Vaseline on your pinky finger and massage its asshole. I'm only doing what the veterinarian gets paid two hundred dollars to do. I just don't feel like paying a quack to whore himself out to my cat," Del replied.

I knew he was trying to shock me, but I usually refrained from reacting. This time I couldn't help myself.

"Let's go back to you yelling at me. I'd rather have you scream at me than listen to you discuss your sexual exploits with cats," I told him.

Del turned to me and shook his head. "If you're going to fuck a cat, fuck a cat. But he was doing it because he thought he was cute and would get a laugh. I don't have time for cuteness," he said.

It was interesting to see exactly what would offend Del. He could find the vilest and most contemptible actions appropriate as long as they respected to his art form.

"I told the class that the whole day had been an exercise in futility, that they were damaged and should rethink their careers in improvisation," he grumbled.

I looked at him and laughed. He wasn't joking.

We did his errands and talked about Bill Clinton, but he continued being angry with me. He was upset with what he considered my lack of commitment. I was worried about my classes. I wondered how they were going to be affected.

I had been doing theater and improv for years now and had discovered that improvisers were an interesting breed. Theater in college and in Chicago had taught me to have thick skin. Many of my theater directors had been pretty demonstrative, fairly frequently berating and abusing the players. Theater actors also go through the process of consistently auditioning and being rejected for roles.

In my experience, most sports coaches were the same way. I had played baseball and soccer throughout my life, and it was pretty common for coaches to yell and scream to get their point across. I never thought my directors or coaches disliked me or doubted my abilities. It was just the way they expressed their opinions.

At that time most of the improvisers from ImprovOlympic hadn't had collegiate or professional theater experience. A great part of improvisational training is based on support and security. Classes through ImprovOlympic had concentrated on instruction and tried to stay away from too much negativity. Some instructors would point out mistakes that students made when they occurred, but they would quickly follow any negative criticism with a positive direction. That style of teaching salvaged the feelings of the students and kept their confidence high.

Del, on the other hand, didn't have time for students' feelings or their confidence. He was blunt and direct, two approaches that sometimes were difficult for students to handle. While athletes and theater actors would rebound from this sometimes volatile instruction, improvisers would recoil and withdraw.

Negative notes from Del brought improvisers to the brink of career suicide. I'd seen many people crushed by Del's comments; in the following weeks they never returned.

Del's opinions mattered. People cared what he thought about them. He was the spiritual leader of this gigantic, loyal community, and people desperately wanted his approval. Whether they liked him or not, they wanted him to like them.

"They needed to hear it," he said. "They'll be better and stronger because of it."

"What if they don't come back?" I asked.

"Fuck 'em," he replied.

The next day, ImprovOlympic called to notify me that the majority of my class had dropped out. Saturday's Performance Class would be combined with Sunday's so that we would have enough people. I called Del and told him about the dropouts.

"It's for the best," he said, "They were severely damaged. Even though there were people missing, they should have been able to cope." As an afterthought, he added, "I'm sure they'll forgive you someday for fucking up their improv careers."

I told him I thought they would probably blame him more than me.

"These are yours," he cackled. "Keep track. I'm sure there will be more."

21

Confidants

"I want to get a laser pointer for my cat," Del mumbled as we drove our normal route to the bank.

It was cold. Bitter cold. El Niño had been keeping the winter fairly pleasant, but this was still Chicago, and February was the harshest month of the season.

The heater was pumping in the truck, but the defroster in the driver's side window was blocked. I had to lean a bit to the right to try to look out Del's window while I was driving. I needed to get that fixed.

"What's your cat going to do with a laser pointer?" I asked him.

"It's not actually for the cat. It's for me to play with the cat, nimrod," he answered.

The windshield wipers scraped off the layers of frost, but the wipers were pretty worn and there were streaks all along the window.

Del had barely uttered a word since he flopped himself into the truck. He was in a pretty depressed mood.

As we pulled up to the bank, Del reached for the door and then settled back without opening it. I looked at him to see if there was any hint as to why he was acting so pensive.

"Who's your best friend?" he asked.

It caught me off guard. Our conversations were pretty deep when it came to Del and improv and current events, but my own life was rarely discussed. I wasn't opposed to talking about myself, but I really didn't offer anything unless it was to answer a direct request. Del loved to talk about himself; his life was an open book. Mine wasn't.

"Mike and Jackie are my best friends," I answered.

"From class?" Del asked, and I nodded. I could see he was thinking. After a few minutes he let out what he had wanted to say: "All my friends are dead."

With that he opened the door and walked to the bank. As the wind whipped around, he slapped his hand to his head to keep his beret from blowing away. He ended up knocking himself upside the head while his hat went flying. He chased after it before finally stepping on it to keep it from blowing farther.

He reached down to pick it up and sheepishly glanced at me to see if I'd witnessed his little slapstick display. Normally I would have laughed like a hyena and rolled down the window and made fun of him, but it wasn't fun to taunt him when he was depressed.

"Angry Del," however, was fun to tease. He'd get mad and yell, and you felt like you'd been given a pretty good show.

"Depressed Del" was one quip away from opening up a vein.

Once Del settled back into the truck he began talking about the "X-Files." I steered the conversation back to his remark about all his friends being dead. I listed two dozen people that Del had told me were good, close friends of his.

Del sighed. "Not including Charna, only two or three of those people have talked to me more than a handful of times in the past five years. And one of those two or three people calls me once a month to borrow money."

We drove in silence as Del chewed on his lip. I wanted to talk about it more, but I didn't want to push too hard.

All of a sudden, he just let it out. The dam had broken and a constant stream of thought flowed through.

"All of those people are good friends that have now turned into acquaintances. They've all moved on, and I'm barely a memory to them. Even the students move on. I mentor them and develop friendships, but they move away and I'm forgotten again. It's great to have them become successful and then have them say nice things about me and give me all kinds of credit for their accomplishments, but I'd almost rather have them come to the theater and sit down and have a conversation with me. I'd settle for a fucking phone call every once in a while. For Christ sake, there's plenty to talk about. We've got a fucking pervert in the White House that can't keep his dick in his pants. Let's talk about that."

Through his entire rant, he kept his eyes forward and his voice steady. There was a complete lack of emotion to his voice.

"I don't blame them. They all have their new lives. They don't want the kook hanging around scaring their new wives and children. I understand that. It's just kind of sad. It used to be that you would share a roach clip or a bowl with someone and that would cement a bond that would last forever."

We talked for a while about Severn Darden and how Del felt that Severn was the greatest friend of his life. Unfortunately Severn had died in 1995, and the only person who had come close to taking his place for Del was the folksinger Jamie Swise. Jamie, a wonderful singer, had been Del's sidekick for many years. Anytime Del was in trouble, Jamie would get a phone call. Sometimes it would be from Del, sometimes it would be from Second City. Someone would spot Del lying in the snow in his underwear at two in the afternoon, and Jamie would get a call to wrangle him in. While Del continued on his wild, reckless path, Jamie fell in love and became the father of a beautiful baby girl. Once that happened, the relationship between Jamie and Del became distant.

"Jamie and I just ran out of things to say," Del said.

He was very fond of the Murray brothers, Bill and Brian Doyle, and felt they had stayed close to him through the years. But now Del was sixty-two, and many of his friends had died. They had lived hard lives, not the least of their difficulty brought on by abuse they wreaked on themselves.

While Del alternated between his bipolar extremes, his slides into misery weren't unjustified. Something usually triggered his move.

As we parked the truck in the parking lot of the Petsmart at Halsted and Clark, Del confided to me about what had upset him. "I realized this morning that I don't have anyone I can talk with when I need to make important decisions, and I have a pretty important decision I have to make," Del said as we made our way to the front door. "I have Charna and I have you. She's too busy, and you keep trying to kill me. It's pretty pathetic."

We were both embarrassed by his last statement. While the two of us had developed an interesting relationship, it was odd to think of us as friends. I had known him for all of three months. During most of that time we had antagonized and irritated each other.

Technically, I worked for him. He and Charna employed me as Del's assistant. There was no way I should have been considered his confidant, but he was a lonely old man who had been abandoned and forgotten by his friends. By default I would now shoulder the role of intimate friend.

"So," he started again, "if you don't mind, I need your advice on something."

Del leaned against the cart and pointed at cat food that he wanted to put in the basket. "Bob Falls is directing *Death of a Salesman* at the Goodman. He called me this morning and asked me to come in and read for him. He wants me to play the part of Uncle Ben." He paused to wait for my reaction.

I was excited for him. Brian Dennehy had been selected to play the part of Willy Loman, and this would be an amazing opportunity for Del. It was no secret that the Goodman Theatre was prepping the show to take it to New York for a run on Broadway.

"I just don't know that I can do it," Del said. "There's a boxing scene in one of the dream sequences, and physically I can't handle it."

I looked at Del with confusion. "You're not thinking about turning it down, are you? That boxing scene can be manipulated, I would think."

Del nodded. "That's what Bob Falls said, but I don't want to disturb the integrity of the piece by having some slow-footed old man with emphysema playing the role."

I stepped in front of the cart and stopped us in the middle of the cat toy aisle. "Del, it sounds like you're making excuses to keep from doing this. I've never heard you make excuses for anything. Why are you doing it now?" He shrugged his shoulders.

He didn't want me to talk him into doing it, he wanted me to tell him that his decision not to do it was correct. I wasn't going to do that. I wanted him to take the role.

I wasn't going to budge from my initial reaction, so Del turned his attention away from me and started looking at the cat toys. "I told him I didn't think I could physically do it, but he told me to come in and do the reading anyway."

I couldn't believe what he was telling me. I put my hands to my face and rubbed my forehead.

He continued, "Besides, I wouldn't want to leave Charna in a bad position. Who would teach my classes if I were to do this play? And, I don't know if I have it in me to take on something new. Rehearsals and previews and all the traveling. I've settled into a pretty nice routine, and this would really disrupt it."

I knew he was using Charna as an excuse. She was very open to him taking on acting jobs. She encouraged it.

I knew what I was about to say would make him mad, but I said it anyway. "Are you scared?"

I expected him to swear at me, but he looked at me sheepishly again. I could tell he was embarrassed. He didn't answer. He didn't have to.

I moved from the front of the cart and walked toward the checkout counter. Del followed. Neither of us spoke.

We walked next door to Walgreens where we wandered around looking for a laser pointer. There were two or three different models that we silently compared. We made our way back to the pharmacy and settled into our familiar seats in the waiting area. It was empty while we sat quietly waiting for Del's medications.

After several minutes, Del broke the silence. "If I were to take the role, you would have to come and work as my assistant full time. You would have to work throughout rehearsals and through the entire run. If I do this, you have to be ready to take on that responsibility."

I sighed, "I'm the one that's scared now. That's way too much time for us to be around each other."

The pharmacist called Del's name and gave us prescriptions for his emphysema, blood pressure, and arthritis. We would pick up the rest of his prescriptions the following week. We made our way out the door. Once we settled into the truck, Del finally addressed my question.

"I'll admit, I'm a little scared. I just wonder if I'm too old to do this anymore. I haven't done a play since *Picasso at the Lapin Agile*."

I was pushing him to take the part. Perhaps I really shouldn't have. There was no doubt in my mind that it was a wonderful opportunity for him. But then again, I had ignored the fact that he was over sixty years old and was very sick from emphysema. His last production at the Goodman had required him to use a cart to make it across the stage.

I apologized. "I'm sorry I questioned you."

He nodded and waved his hand at me not to worry about it. "I'll need help. Physically and mentally."

We rambled through the slick, cold streets and arrived at Del's apartment. His audition with the Goodman was scheduled for the following day. He promised to call to let me know how it had gone.

The call never came.

Several days later, during a break in our class, I approached Del and asked him how the reading had gone. He walked over to the ashtray and poked around to find some half-smoked cigarette butts. He found a butt that was an eighth the size of a regular cigarette. He put it in his pocket and looked at me for the first time.

"I went to the audition and told them before I started reading that I thought it would be impossible for me to take the role. Bob Falls tried to talk me into changing my mind, but I told him I just didn't think it would work out," Del said as we stood in the hallway of the downstairs theater in ImprovOlympic.

After the rest of the class filed in, Del walked to the table next to the piano in front of the stage. I stood and watched him address the class. He had returned to his normal, confident, intimidating presence.

I was annoyed at him for not taking the part. I was mad at myself for not pushing him to do it.

In the late eighties, Del had played the role of Ozzie Mandeus on a syndicated TV show called "My Talk Show," filmed in L.A. Once a show, Ozzie would take over the airwaves and spout out a monologue about topics ranging from windup Jesus dolls to the death penalty. One particular monologue had Del preaching to senior generations throughout the world. His grainy image pleaded and whispered to the camera, "Do not go gentle into that good night. Rage, rage against the dying of the light."

I was frustrated because I didn't think he was following his own advice. I should have realized that he was sicker than I thought.

22

Second City—The Initial Voyage

Del's first stint with Second City began in 1961. Paul Sills, a co-founder and the company's primary director, had a sometimes volatile relationship with the cast. The other producers worried that Sills was losing interest in putting together the shows. A few months after Second City opened its doors, a disagreement flared. Del was brought in to smooth over the discord.

Del handled workshops with the cast. The threat of having him waiting in the wings prompted Sills to ease up with the performers. Sills still yelled and screamed at them, but having Del around, ready to take over, sparked his competitive nature. He channeled his aggression and focused it on production.

Del was soon moved next door to Second City's Playwrights Theater, where he performed and directed in Jules Feiffer's show *The Beginners* and David Shepherd's *The Big Deal* with Alan Arkin and Avery Schreiber. Soon after those productions ended, Del moved to the main stage of Second City and joined the cast as a performer.

He stayed there directing and acting for four years. When Sills grew restless, Del would step in and finish the work. Second City was still in its infancy, and its performers considered their jobs only temporarily stable. The doors stayed open and the theater fared well at the box office, but their earlier Compass experiences left the cast skeptical.

While Del found a measure of stability in Chicago at Second City, his pal Lenny Bruce was being arrested for saying "cocksucker" during a performance at the Jazz Workshop in San Francisco. Bruce's trials, challenging obscenity laws, made headlines around the country. Del and Second City began pushing the boundaries themselves as their humor grew racier and more political.

Because his first comedy album had done well, Del followed it with *How to Speak Hip*, a guide for squares recorded with John Brent, also of Second City. On the album, Brent plays Geets Romo, a hipster who consents to guide the square interviewer, Close, through the basic lexicon of hip.

After a 1962 Second City trip to London for a show at the Establishment Club in Soho, Del contracted hepatitis and was bedridden for an extended time. When he rejoined Second City, his erratic behavior worsened as his successes grew. Theater people recognized his immeasurable talent but wearied of his antics. He became the bad boy and rebel of Second City.

For Del, drugs became a daily activity. While other cast members would stay up to all hours of the night talking literature and politics, Del would disappear for a few hours so that he could take any illegal substance he could get his hands on.

And his mood swings were becoming destructive. He attempted suicide on two different occasions. Afterward, for his safety, doctors institutionalized him. Members of the cast had to pick him up at the sanitarium each day before the show. Once stabilized, he was released and became a functioning member of society again. But he began noticing that cast members were looking at him again out of the corner of their eye. It was the same look he remembered from his childhood in Manhattan, Kansas. They were wondering what he was about to do next.

Although he was unstable and emotionally precarious, Del was considered a brilliant performer and director. Second City put up with him because they believed his talent outweighed his capricious behavior. When Paul Sills took an extended leave to concentrate on other projects, Alan Myerson assumed directing duties. A disagreement between Del and Myerson over material that was being rehearsed led to a showdown. Del suggested that Myerson was an inadequate, amateurish director, and Myerson confronted him. So Del went to the producers with an ultimatum. "It's me or him," he told them. Myerson was moved to direct the Second City's show in New York; Sills was brought back to direct the main stage.

For the next few years Del shuffled between directing and acting. Notably, he was the first person to drop the dreaded "F-bomb" on Second City's stage. The day after President Kennedy was assassinated, Del prompted the audience to supply him with a suggestion for the improv set. A gentleman shouted, "The assassination," to which Del responded, "Just what the fuck did you want to see, sir?" The audience roared with applause.

Del directed several revues in his first four-year stint at Second City and brought to them a unique perspective. But his drug problems finally made it impossible for Second City to continue to employ him. A line was drawn in the sand when the producers told Del that he would be fired if he didn't get his drug problem under control.

He didn't. He was fired from Second City in 1965.

23

Birthdays and Suicide

How had he made it to sixty-three years of age?

He'd spent four and a half decades abusing his body with alcohol, drugs, and cigarettes with a veracity that had already put many of his friends in the grave. Many times he said it was getting increasingly embarrassing that he was still alive.

But he was surviving them all—John Belushi, Gilda Radner, Don Depollo, John Candy, Lenny Bruce, Severn Darden. The list was growing longer as the years progressed.

Del was very fond of Don Depollo, a performer and teacher at Second City. When Don died in 1995, Del was one of the many dignitaries who were invited to speak at the Second City memorial service. A loving and humorous retrospective of Don's life was presented by his friends and family. Toward the end of the ceremony, Del arose to eulogize his friend. "Before we continue canonizing Saint Depollo, I'd like to say that I find it interesting that no one has mentioned the hookers or the cocaine," he said, to the shock of the roomful of mourners. In his tactless way, he suggested that such memorials shouldn't be used as a way to exalt the recently departed. Morally, people may have disagreed with the drugs and the prostitutes, he said, but leaving them out wouldn't be a proper commemoration.

I imagined what Del would say at his own funeral as I walked up to his apartment. He opened the door and shouted, "I'm not dressed yet, Firecracker. Come in and drink some tea." He was walking around barefoot, wearing a black T-shirt and jeans. The apartment was a mess, as usual. Crumpled newspapers and boxes were everywhere. Three or four boxes had arrived with birthday gifts. Most of them were books.

I sat down at the kitchen table, and Del placed a coffee mug in front of me. Amazingly, it looked clean. He opened a new bag of Lipton tea and dropped it in the mug. I thought I might actually drink the tea this time. It was a freezing March afternoon, and a cup of hot tea would be warming.

I plopped on the table a paper bag I had brought with me. Del eyed it as he poured the steaming water into my mug. I put my hands around the cup and let the heat warm them.

Del knew I had brought a gift for him, but he acted nonchalant about it. He sat down in front of the bag and put on his socks and boots. I could tell it was eating him alive to know what was in the bag.

The fact that he had survived his own demons was astounding. The tale of Del's last moments with his father is legendary and vintage Del. It plays out like folklore, and the controversy and confusion surrounding it is vintage Del as well.

According to Del, when he was a child his father had brought him into the kitchen and sat at the dinner table. "I want you to see something son," he had said as he placed a glass on the table in front of the both of them. After a few minutes of talking to his son about his poetry magazine, his father reached forward and turned the glass slowly. It was filled with a clear liquid, but it didn't look like water. It was too thick.

His father then deliberately and quietly drank the liquid. It was the first time his father had expressed interest in any of

Del's projects. They talked a few minutes more about the poems that were being included in the current issue of the magazine. Del waited for his father to respond, but it became difficult for Del Sr. to speak. The son sat in his seat and watched his father die. The glass had been filled with jewelry cleaning acid.

While it was certain that Del's father had killed himself, it is uncertain when it happened or if Del was even there. The story of his father's death had changed over the years, with many different versions floating around. While the version Del related to me had him as a child, his age fluctuated each time he told the story.

An obituary from the *Manhattan Mercury* reports that Del's father died on December 16, 1954, at the Mercy Health Center. Del Sr. had been discovered unconscious and alone in the family jewelry store, the result of a self-inflicted injury. The newspaper reported that Del Jr. was at his father's bedside in the hospital when his father died. He would have been twenty years old and living in New York at the time.

It's a mystery why Del exaggerated the story of his father's death. It only reinforced people's questions about his mental health.

"Suicide is hereditary," Del often told me. "I just didn't get as severe a case as my father had."

By "severe" he meant that he couldn't carry it through. He kept trying to kill himself, but he couldn't get the final step right. If he was going to be bad at something, suicide was a good candidate.

I was intrigued by his suicide attempts. Anytime they came up in conversation, I asked him about them. His suicide stories were chilling and disturbing, and I couldn't resist wanting to hear about them.

"I can't believe you've never thought about killing yourself," he would always say. "How did you become so arrogant that you never questioned the futility of your existence?"

Each time I told him that killing myself had never entered my mind, it angered him more. He would call me a "self-centered, self-indulgent, arrogant bastard."

While I had never considered taking my life, suicide was something I had spent a great deal of time thinking about. I confessed to Del that my great-grandmother had killed herself when I was a child. She was sixty-six. I was seven. My family and I had been planning to visit her that afternoon. A little party had been planned for my mother's birthday.

"Was she your mother's grandmother or your dad's?" Del asked when I told him.

"My mother's grandmother," I responded.

"What a fucking birthday gift," Del groaned. "How did she do it?"

I shook my head and told him, "Twelve-gauge shotgun."

"Jesus," Del whispered as his eyes opened wide. "The old bitch was serious."

When we had arrived at my great-grandparents' house, my great-grandfather had walked us through the events of the morning. It was 1978, and they lived in Fishhook, Illinois. Their house had no indoor plumbing; he had gone to the outhouse. A few minutes after the wooden door of the outhouse banged shut, he heard a gunshot and went running back to the house. She had walked to the back storage room, taken the shotgun off the rack, and put the barrel in her mouth. She knew my great-grandfather kept the gun loaded, so it was ready and waiting for her. She squeezed the trigger and blew a hole through the back of her head.

We were outside standing next to the storage room. I could see the hole in the wall where the shotgun blast had exited. I leaned forward to sneak a peek inside through the window. The coroner had come and taken the body, but there was a gigantic pool of blood on the floor. This was small Pike County. They cleaned up after their own.

After I told Del this story, he felt we had a common bond. He told me all his suicide stories. My stomach would grow queasy as I listened to him describe every detail. Most of his attempts involved overdoses with needles and pills, but he also toyed around with razors and knives.

I sipped the tea and felt the heat slide down my throat. Del kept his eye on the bag I had placed on the table as he asked, "How does it taste?"

"It's good," I answered.

I nodded my head toward the bag, "That's for you. Happy Birthday."

"Lookie, lookie," he said, like a little kid. He had a fascination with brains and skulls, so I had bought him a glow-in-the-dark skull and a rubber brain that oozed puss and blood when you squeezed it.

"This is great," he kept muttering as he sat at the table playing with his new toys.

The apartment was fully stocked with cat food and groceries, so we headed to the Mongolian BBQ where I wanted to treat him to a birthday lunch. Afterward we made our way to the picture frame shop on Clybourn so he could get some show posters framed.

"This has been a pretty good last birthday," he said as we sat in some wonderfully upholstered chairs waiting for his posters to be finished.

I rolled my eyes. "You keep saying that just so you can sound prophetic. After you die, you want everyone to say, 'Oh my God. He was so right. He totally predicted that this was going to be his last Arbor Day.'"

"Fuck off," he chuckled.

Del suddenly became nostalgic and waxed on about his birthdays through the years. Initially the stories were pleasant, but one unsettling reminiscence portrayed a pretty unhappy birthday.

The employees of the deserted frame store pretended to work as they listened to Del tell how he was living at the Old Town Inn, just a few blocks from Second City where he was working. In a cocaine haze he had decided to kill himself and had pulled out a straight razor and steadied his hands in an effort to cut his wrists.

As he placed the razor against his skin, he paused for one final resolve before he made the slice. He closed his eyes and gathered his thoughts. When he opened his eyes he realized that he'd blanked out for a few moments. The interval had calmed him, and he no longer wanted to end his life.

When he saw his arms covered in blood, his mind raced to try to understand what had happened. Everything was foggy. He couldn't figure out if he'd made a cut while he was blacked out, or if this was all a delusion.

Now the blood was dripping everywhere. Del realized he should get help and worry later about how it happened. He went to the phone and took it off the hook, but the blood all over his hand caused the phone to slip and fall to the floor. He kept trying to pick it up but couldn't get a grip on it. Finally he did. He had a rotary phone and dialed the only number he could remember at the time.

Jamie Swise answered the phone. Del recited the line that so many of his friends had heard before: "Jamie, it's Del. I've gone and done it again. I need some help."

Jamie had been through this exercise numerous times and had reached his breaking point. "Del," he hollered into the phone, "I'm tired of your bullshit attempts to get attention. If you're going to kill yourself, do us all a favor and really do it this time."

And with that, Jamie hung up.

The bloody phone slipped out of Del's paw as he slumped against the wall. He couldn't pick it up. He laid his head on the floor and nestled it against the phone. He tried to dial the number for Second City, but his fingers kept sliding out of the dial holes.

The phone was impossible to use now, so he decided to leave his apartment and get help in the lobby of his apartment building. He stood up and immediately fell down. The loss of blood had made him dizzy. Everything around him was spinning. As he lay on the ground he could taste blood dripping into his throat.

He couldn't believe this was how he was going out. He'd killed himself and couldn't remember doing it.

The light faded as he drifted into darkness.

The next morning he opened his eyes and sat up. There was blood everywhere. He looked down at his arms and saw that the blood had dried on his wrist.

For a few moments he thought he had awoken in the afterworld. "Holy shit," he thought, "I'm in Valhalla and it's still this same fucking apartment."

After his head cleared, he stood up and walked to the bathroom. He looked at his reflection in the mirror and was shocked to see that blood was caked and matted all over his face and clothes. Peering in closer, he discovered that it was coming from his nose. He had busted a capillary in his nostril from the cocaine.

He took a rag and some cleaning solution and wiped up the blood that was covering the floor and walls. The phone took a little extra time to clean. After he was finished cleaning the apartment, he jumped into the shower and washed himself.

In the warm shower, a feeling of relief spread throughout his body. The cocaine had intensified his feelings of despair and had pushed him to try to kill himself. Now that his mind was clear, he remembered his conversation with Jamie from the night before. Del had become an annoyance and a joke to his friends; he was embarrassed they felt that way.

Jamie's words had hurt. There was only one thing for him to do. He dried himself off, put on a fresh set of clothes, went to the phone, and dialed the nearest hospital. He told them that in ten minutes he was going to take a bottle of pills and they needed to send an ambulance.

When the operator advised him not to take the pills, he answered, "Well, I don't want to, but now I have to, just for spite."

I laughed, and the frame store employees looked shocked that we were laughing.

Del's frames were ready, so we took them back to his home. I hung up his posters around the apartment. He was eating dinner with a friend later that evening, so I wished him a happy birthday and started for the door.

He thanked me for the gift and reached his hand out for me to shake it. When I did, he pulled me in slightly and patted me on the back with his left hand.

"I think we just hugged," I thought to myself. I giggled to myself as I walked out of the apartment.

24

Comedy's Unabomber

Improv had grown. Immensely. The mid-nineties had been a boon to improvisation as entertainment. "Who's Line Is It Anyway?", a successful TV program in the United Kingdom, was based on short-form improv games. The comedian Drew Carey adapted the program for the United States and enjoyed a prosperous run on the ABC Network.

Aspiring actors and directors traveled to New York for theater, to Los Angeles for movies, and now to Chicago for comedy. The Second City theater drew people from throughout the country who wanted to study at the venue that had groomed comedy legends like Bill Murray, Shelley Long, John Belushi, Dan Aykroyd, Gilda Radner, John Candy, and George Wendt. Second City also now had three touring companies traversing the world, entertaining and introducing improvisation to people from all walks of life.

With Del's legend growing and celebrities like Chris Farley and Mike Myers trumpeting the importance of its training, ImprovOlympic too had established itself as a major force. Improv clubs from around the country began inviting Del to visit their cities and teach them what he'd been workshopping in Chicago. He began bringing students with him from Improv-Olympic so they could illustrate the ideas and philosophies he was preaching.

Some innovative improvisers began promoting Del's visits as events, inviting nearby improv groups and communities to take part in the classes and performances. What began as afternoon classes with a reputable instructor from Chicago turned into weeklong festivals featuring teachers and improv groups from around the world.

The Big Stinkin' Improv Festival was the biggest of the bunch. It took place in Austin, Texas, and attracted hundreds of performers and teachers. The festival also became hugely popular because casting agents and producers made the trek to the Texas city, on the prowl for fresh talent. An invitation to Austin was coveted.

Del had been working with one of his recent classes to develop a form he was quite proud of. The class members were called the Lindbergh Babies, and they performed dual monologues. Del was scheduled to teach at the Austin festival; the Lindbergh Babies had applied to be one of the performing teams.

The festival organizers asked for promotional material and newspaper reviews along with the application. The Lindbergh Babies could have relied on their connection with Del to get an invitation, but they wanted to be included in the festival on their own merit. So they invited a reviewer from the *Chicago Reader*, an alternative free weekly, to attend one of their shows.

Del and I had been tipped off that the grocery store at Clark and Division received its bundles of the *Reader* earlier than most other locations. We sat in the truck the next Thursday and waited for the white van to pull into the parking lot and drop off the paper.

"It was a good show," Del mumbled to me as he anxiously pulled on his beard. "I'll be pretty disappointed if the review's bad." I hadn't seen the show, so I didn't have an opinion.

As the van pulled up, Del jumped out of the truck and raced to the doors of the grocery store. The newspaper men pulled two shopping carts up to the side of the van and unloaded fifty copies into each one. The newspaper stacks were bundled into groups of ten, a thick yellow plastic band wound tightly around each bunch.

I watched Del futilely try to pull one of the newspapers out of its pack. He couldn't get it out and was growing frustrated. When his hand went into his pocket, I knew what he was doing. The flame of his lighter flashed as Del tried to maneuver the lighter so that it touched only the plastic banding. After a few minutes his hand began swatting to extinguish the fire he had inevitably started.

He returned the lighter to his pocket and disappeared into the store. He was antsy. He had been talking all day about the review. He couldn't wait for it to come out. Within minutes he reappeared with some scissors. He cut the band, tossing the scissors aside. Standing at the shopping cart, he pulled out section two, the theater reviews. He tossed the other sections back onto the pile and began scouring for the review.

I watched from the truck and tried to gauge his reaction. I had decided that if it was a bad review, I was going to slide the gearshift into drive and head out of there. He could find his own way home. Suddenly Del's fist thrust into the air. He grabbed two more copies and almost jogged to the passenger door.

"This is great!" he exclaimed as he jumped into the cab of the truck. He was giddy. "Let me read it to you," he said as I slid out of the parking lot. I turned on the dome light because it was four o'clock and dusk had arrived.

ImprovOlympic had packaged the Lindbergh Babies show with a form that Charna had created called the Living Room. Del read:

"The differences between ImprovOlympic partners Charna Halpern and Del Close are nowhere more apparent than in these two shows. Where Halpern is all warmth, smiles, and clearheaded competence, dispensing free drinks and pointed maternal wisdom, Close is the quintessential portrait of the artist as an old grouch, with a twisted, radical genius that's made him the Ted Kaczynski of modern comedy."

Kaczynski had recently been arrested as the long-sought-after "unabomber." Del couldn't be happier. He was called a radical genius, and he was pleased.

"Close's 'Show,' performed by the Lindbergh Babies, contains fewer laughs but infuses its subjects with such insane inspiration that the evening is a consistent, hypnotic delight, never slowing until the final blackout. Beginning with purportedly autobiographical monologues and moving into an increasingly complex pattern of scenes based on a song title provided by the audience, the Lindbergh Babies on the night I attended puzzled and at times alienated the audience with their leaps into the realm of meteorology, astronomy, and chemistry. These exceedingly intelligent, gifted performers made 'The Living Room' seem predictable and sophomoric by comparison; such is the difference between technical proficiency and mad genius."

"Could you ask for a better review?" Del gleamed as we sat in his kitchen reading the review for what seemed like the hundredth time. He reached for the phone to call Charna.

After exchanging pleasantries, Del read Charna the review, gratuitously rereading the part that called him Ted Kaczynski. "It's good publicity for the theater. He called me the mad scientist of improv, isn't that great?" he excitedly asked her.

He was silent for a few minutes and his brow furrowed. I could tell from his reaction that she wasn't as pleased about the review. Overall it was very favorable to her show but had also commented that "this somewhat seasick show is far too comfortable with itself."

He rolled his eyes and handed me one of his copies of the review. "Take these to Kinko's and get some copies made. I'll get them from you when we have class this weekend."

The unabomber had just given me my orders. This was the worst example of someone believing their press. If I didn't get it right, I might get a letter in the mail.

25

Spoo

Del had encouraged me to take classes with Mick Napier at the Annoyance Theater because he was very fond of him. I unloaded his groceries and told him I was getting a little confused with the different styles of teaching.

"It's good for you to learn the different styles," he told me. "I don't want you to think there's only one way to do things. I get frustrated with all these performers and teachers who are so arrogant they feel they're too good to learn from someone else. Too many performers and teachers think they know everything. They don't do anything to try to get better. The problem with that thinking is, this fucking thing keeps changing."

"When we first started doing the Harold," he began, "we improvised with plot in mind. It's changed now. Plot is no longer necessary and usually gets in the way of exploration. The Harold now is based around relationships, not plot. I don't want to see two people in the first scene talking about doing a bank robbery, then in the second scene see them arrive at the bank, and the third scene has them finally robbing the bank. I'd rather see them working as tellers at the bank in the second scene because they've decided to give up bank robbing. The third scene could show the two of them working in Fort Knox.

The relationship is the cornerstone of the Harold. Plot just gets in the way."

Scruthers was jumping around on top of the cabinet making me nervous. There was no telling what disgusting treasure he had hidden up there. Del continued to talk as I stepped away from the cabinet before the cat could toss anything he'd captured onto me.

"It would be antiquated for us to keep teaching the same exercises and the same lessons that Charna and I taught when we opened ImprovOlympic fifteen years ago. Improvisation constantly changes and evolves. It changes so quickly that it will all pass you by, and you won't see that you've been left behind until it's too late. Unless teachers and performers continue to take classes and learn from each other, they'll find themselves deserted and ignored by a populace that yearns to explore and learn from instructors who continue to grow. Everyone needs to understand that this is an art form that grows and changes at the same acceleration and in the same manner that our society and culture grow and change."

I finished telling Del about my class with Mick. He interrupted me a few times to ask me questions. I really liked Mick's class and felt I was learning a great deal. Some of Mick's theories contradicted Del's, but I was able to find a comfortable middle ground between the two styles.

Earlier in the year Del had gone to Kansas City to teach at the Kansas City Improv Festival. The teachers had each taken a group of performers to develop a form. Del put together one that manipulated and bastardized the Harold; he felt it went well.

Mick's form had blown Del away. It was reminiscent of a Greek chorus, Del said. It had grabbed Del "by the collar and had tossed him aside like a toy doll."

Del had been humbled by how much better Mick's show had been. I was impressed by how Del handled it. He announced to all his classes and to anyone who would listen that Mick Napier had beaten him at his own game.

For some reason Del had fallen in love with the word "Spoo" and asked us if our class would call ourselves that for our show. We said, "Whatever." The form we used for our show was inspired by the one that Mick had used in Kansa City. In three weeks I would be in my first show directed by Del Close.

26

Belts

Del was a few days away from leaving for Austin, Texas, to take part in the third annual Big Stinkin' Improv Festival. He was downright giddy.

He loved the festivals. They pampered him. They worshiped him. Everyone lived and breathed long-form improv for a week, and Del became more than just a teacher. He became their leader.

"I'm bigger than Jesus at these fucking things," he said to me as we went through his itinerary for the week.

He'd asked if I wanted to go with him so that I could help him out while he was down there, but I had already planned on visiting my parents that weekend. The festival coordinators had arranged to have someone assist Del the entire time he was there, so I didn't feel bad.

We sat in a booth at a Mexican restaurant as Del prattled on about earlier festivals he had attended in Austin. The highlight for him each year was to go to the bridge at dusk and watch the bats fly into the sunset. Del waxed on about the bats and even flapped his arms as he pretended to fly to the restroom. When he came back, I noticed his belt for the first time.

It was mid-March, and the weather was amazingly pleasant. Both of us had worn jackets, but we ditched them as soon as we stepped into the diner.

In the restroom Del had tucked his South Park T-shirt into his pants, which was why I hadn't noticed his belt earlier. Around his waist he had run a rope through his belt loops and tied the ends into a knot in front.

"What are you looking at?" he growled at me as he stood at the table.

"I see you've jumped into the Texas hillbilly spirit early, Uncle Jed."

"I broke my belt this morning, shithead. Shut the fuck up. That's one of our errands today. We have to buy me a new belt."

Del continued standing at the edge of the table. I couldn't stop smirking at how ridiculous he looked.

"Be careful," I joked, "you're going to get your rope in the food."

He sat back down in the booth. "You're so fucking funny," he said.

Every time I looked at him, I laughed.

"I'll tell you," he started, "one reason I'm glad I'm getting out of this town is because I need a break from you. Your bullshit gets old quick."

This made me laugh harder. We didn't speak for the rest of the meal. I tried, but each time I started I would begin laughing. Del didn't even try.

We went to Marshall's on Belmont and Clark and searched for a leather belt. I found one for him, but he thought it looked too "gay." It was a leather woven belt; he could tie it like his rope. He thought I was making fun of him, so he refused to get it.

"When I was younger, I'd use a piece of rope instead of a belt all the time," he barked at me as we waited to pay for his items.

"Did you have a 'work rope' and a 'fancy-go-to-church-meetin-rope,' or did you have just one rope for all occasions?"

"Fuck it," he said, tossing his new belt on the floor. He walked past the cash registers and took the escalator down to the lobby.

I walked over and picked up the belt and paid for it. Del was waiting at the revolving door as I descended the escalator. I handed him the bag and he took it. He didn't offer to pay me back.

We drove home while Del chewed his lip in the passenger seat. When we arrived at his apartment, he sat for a second without talking or moving.

He spoke very quietly, but his voice was menacing. "It was very fashionable to wear a rope for a belt. I was very handsome when I was younger, and I looked very trendy wearing a rope belt."

I snorted, "I doubt that."

Now he was yelling. "Are you saying that I wasn't good-looking enough to be able to pull off a rope belt? Is that what you're saying?"

I shrugged my shoulders and waited for him to get out of the truck.

"You fucking asshole," he bellowed. "I have tons of pictures that will show you just how handsome I was. I was fucking dashing."

"I'm sure you were, Del," I said in my most patronizing voice.

"You're fucking right I was, and I'll tell you something else: I got more pussy wearing a rope belt than you will ever have in your entire life." He opened the door and crawled out of the cab of the truck. The force with which he slammed the door practically knocked him down.

"Have fun in Texas," I said as he walked to the sidewalk.

"Fuck you," he said as he walked away.

I pulled the truck back into traffic and moved a few feet before stopping at a red light. Waiting for the light to turn green, I laughed to myself. I knew that by the time I got home I would have five messages from Del. The first four would be shockingly abusive, and the last one would be an offer to reconcile. I knew I would call him after the "X-Files" rerun and we'd make up.

The light turned green. I started to put my foot on the gas when I heard Del yelling at the top of his lungs.

"Fucking cocksucker!"

Del was standing in the middle of the sidewalk holding the belt that I had bought him. It was the leather woven one that he had called "gay."

I pulled away and watched in the mirror as he tossed the belt after me. It didn't go very far, and he picked it up and carried it back to his apartment.

I thought I would probably wait and call him the next day.

27

Chats with Cats

Del was back from Texas. He seemed to have had a good time.

By "good time" I mean he must have smoked a lot of pot. He had smoked pretty much every day since his return. We missed two weeks of errands because he was too high to leave his apartment.

The phone calls were always the same and always made me laugh. I would be on my way out the door when the phone would ring. It would be Del.

"I forgot that we were going to run our errands today, and I managed to get myself way too high to be able to do anything. We'll have to cancel this week." I'd offer to pick him up the next day, but he always declined.

Winter had slipped into early spring without anyone noticing. It was the end of March, and it seemed like it had rained every day since mid-February. Del called to say that he was getting really low on supplies for himself and Scruthers. I wasn't busy, so we decided I would go to Del's on Wednesday instead of Thursday.

I got to the apartment and was repulsed as soon as I walked in the door. The place smelled like someone had left a bucket

of blood drying in the sun. Scruthers had given up using the lit-
ter box. Garbage was everywhere. Uneaten Mexican food lay all
around the apartment.

I made a promise to myself that no matter how badly I
needed to use the bathroom, I would refrain. The smells emanating from there were close to what I imagine hell smells like.

I kept my mouth closed and breathed through my nose.
There were some evil germs flying through the air.

Del sat down and started watching TV, so I sat down and
watched it with him. The ever-present cup of tea was missing.
I had brought a soda with me, but I was surprised that Del
hadn't placed a mug in front of me. Maybe he had become wise
to the fact that I was never going to drink it.

Repo Man was showing on TV, and Del was having the time
of his life. The worse the movie got, the harder Del laughed. He
was laughing so hard that he got me laughing.

When the movie ended, I started getting ready to run our
errands. I knew that Del had to go to the bank, and it was getting pretty late in the afternoon to do that.

But Del stayed, flipping through the channels. When the
opening credits for *Raising Arizona* flashed across the scene,
Del put down the remote. He didn't budge. He sat transfixed to
the television. As Nicholas Cage ran through the grocery store
with the diapers, Del mumbled, "This'll be good."

I looked at my watch. The bank was closed; it was getting
late. I'd been there for three hours and we weren't close to getting anything done.

A couple of times we had run our errands and then watched
TV before I headed home, but those had been special cases. I
usually stuck around because he had seemed lonely or because
the weather was too bad outside. Neither of these was the case
today.

I stopped watching the movie and started looking around the apartment. I inventoried everything that needed to be done to get it back into working order. The only way to clean the place completely was to burn it down and start over.

As I was calculating which room would burn the fastest, Del jumped up and screamed at the top of his lungs. I jumped behind the refrigerator because I thought he was going to throw the remote at me.

He squinted at me and finally yelled, "Jeff? When did you get here?"

He was completely baked.

"I've been sitting here for three hours," I yelled back at him.

"I thought you were my cat."

"How could you think I was your cat? We've been sitting at this table talking the entire time I was here."

He smiled and said, "You'd be surprised how many times that cat has talked to me within the past few months."

Del couldn't keep his eyes open. "How high are you?" I asked him.

"I've gotten hold of some very wonderful pot," he said as he put his hand against the back of the chair to steady himself. "Frank gave me some shit that has knocked me off my ass. I don't know what's in it, but I've been having these amazing hallucinations."

I grabbed a pen and wrote a note to him telling him I would come back tomorrow. At the bottom, in big letters, I wrote, "DON'T GET HIGH!" I took a magnet and placed it on the refrigerator.

"I spent all last night talking to this woman Margaret, and guess who came up and talked to us?" he mumbled to me as I walked to the door to leave. I opened it and started down the stairs.

Del followed me a bit and answered his own question. "It was Jesus. You know Jesus. From the Bible. He sat around and we all talked about 'South Park.'"

I stepped outside and stood for a few minutes in the rain. I didn't care that I was getting wet. I just wanted to breathe fresh air and let the raindrops wash away the grime from that ungodly apartment.

I took a deep breath. I'd be back in the abyss again tomorrow.

28

The Point of Conflict

Del greeted me with, "It's not nice to fuck with an old man when he's high."

As we headed to our usual haunts, Del began talking about his trip to Texas. He had taught classes almost every day at the festival, but it had been a bit of a struggle.

"These long-form improvisation teachers are teaching their students to find the 'game of the scene' and the 'point of conflict' in every scene, and it's destroying the art form," he yelled as we walked toward the pet store.

"Congratulations, numb nuts, you found the game of the scene. Now tell me who the two of you are in the scene and what is your goddamn relationship. Improvisation is about being in the moment and moving forward. 'Point of conflict' and always 'finding the game of the scene' doesn't allow anyone to advance and explore relationships. They're up on the stage selling each other out for laughs."

He was upset. This was an art form he had helped create, and it saddened him to think it was devolving into a parlor trick.

"We spend all our time in Chicago nagging at people to do everything possible to keep from arguing. It's disheartening to go to these festivals and reprogram these poor people. These students are being misled by all these assholes who read Keith Johnstone's *Impro* and think they're experts."

I wasn't sure what to say to him. I don't think he wanted me to say anything. I think he just wanted to talk. He had been feeling vulnerable lately and was certainly feeling mortal. He and the other Compass Players had invented and developed this performance form. Del was the only one who had devoted his life to the work, and he felt a great deal of ownership. Mike Nichols was directing movies in Hollywood, and Elaine May was out there too, directing and acting and helping Mike write his films. Bernie Sahlins and Paul Sills had always argued with Del that improvisation was solely an exercise to develop a scripted product. Del was the only one of the old guard who believed in improvisation as a performance form that could stand on its own.

He frowned and raised his eyebrows. "The bats were cool, though. I wish Chicago could find a way to bring those bats up here from Austin."

He turned his attention to the cat food. I prodded him to say a little more, but he was tired of the subject. "I just needed to rant a bit. I fixed as many people as I could. Now it's their job to spread the word to everyone else," he said as he dumped four cans of Tender Vittles into the shopping cart.

I smiled as we made our way to the checkout counter. "You've got yourself a nice little Jesus complex there, Del," I said as I unloaded the cart.

"I'm better than Jesus," he said. "What I say makes sense."

29

The Committee

After Del was fired from The Second City in 1965, an improv company called The Committee brought him to San Francisco. He became resident director and launched the group into intensive theatrical experiments. His dream of improvisation as a theatrical presentation in itself was coming to fruition. It was in San Francisco that he developed and designed the Harold.

The Harold was a performance piece that relied on a single suggestion from the audience. Performers would base the entire show on that one suggestion, weaving story lines, characters, and themes throughout the entire piece. The Harold utilized every tool in the improviser's bag and was created spontaneously with the help of the audience.

The one regret Del had with the Harold was the name itself. When he introduced it, he asked his students, "What'll we call it?" The piano player, Bill Matthews, replied, "Harold." Later, when people asked Del why he had chosen the name, he replied, "Well, the Beatles called their haircut Arthur, so why not call it Harold?" He regretted being so flippant and considered changing the name once he started teaching it in Chicago, but he decided to stick with it to avoid confusion.

The Committee, which included such comedy luminaries as Howard Hesseman, Tiny Tim, Peter Bonerz, and Barbara Bosson, explored the boundaries of established theater conventions. Once the boundaries were discovered, Del liberated the performers to trust and expand the creative spirits to take them beyond the parameters that existed.

"Trust falls" is an exercise demonstrating trust in ensemble work. On one occasion Del demonstrated trust falls by hurling himself off a second-story stage. The jump took the performers by surprise, and when they failed to catch him, he crashed to the stage, breaking his shoulder. So as not to dissuade them from using trust as a major tool, Del went back up the ladder, told them he was going to do it again, and threw himself down with such force that they dropped him a second time.

"He was sensational in that he would commit to ideas," Hesseman said. "He would devise the most outrageous—and, to everyone else, incomprehensible—exercises. But they would foster open-channeled creativity."

Under Del's direction The Committee created material that reflected the country's edgy, uneasy social situation in the late sixties. They were anti-Establishment, and Del was their ringleader. The Committee concentrated on politics and planted themselves fiercely against the government. The drug culture and rebellious protests were in full bloom in San Francisco. Del was right in the middle of them.

The drug problems that had led to his exit from Second City didn't raise a murmur in California. He took heroin, speed, and acid liberally. In a Los Angeles club he and his former roommate, Hugh Romney, also known as Wavy Gravy, performed a show called "Lysergic A-Go-Go." Combining rock music with mind-bending light designs, it became the first commercially publicized event promoting LSD.

When a group known as the Warlocks hired Del to be their lighting technician, he developed a mirage of figures and colors that were called "psychedelic." Thus he earned a credit for the first psychedelic light show. The band changed its name to The Grateful Dead, and Del toured with Jerry Garcia and the rest of the band for several years (the exact dates are unclear).

In December 1969, four months after Woodstock, Del arrived with The Grateful Dead by helicopter at the Altamont, California, motor speedway. The Dead were scheduled to play as a part of a day-long festival in San Francisco that had been organized and headlined by the Rolling Stones. About 300,000 people jammed into the speedway, and the organizers put a group of Hell's Angels in charge of security around the stage. Armed with pool cues and knives, the Angels spent most of the concert beating up spectators. As Jerry Garcia, Del, and members of The Grateful Dead were landing at the event, they could see the chaos on the ground.

"We hit the ground and I told the guys in the band, 'Let's get the fuck back in that whirlybird and get the hell out of here,'" Del recalled. The Grateful Dead left the event soon after arriving and never played at the concert. By the end of the day, three people had been killed and the free-love spirit of the sixties had been spoiled.

While in California, Del also fell in with Ken Kesey and the Merry Pranksters. Kesey had written *One Flew Over the Cuckoo's Nest* and traveled around California promoting large-scale public events called "Acid Tests." Upon entering one of these concerts or festivals, attendees were treated to a cup of "electric Kool-Aid." Kesey and the Pranksters would encourage the participants to drink up, whereupon the entire gathering would trip on LSD.

Avery Schreiber, who had starred at Second City, also studied with Del at The Committee. Schreiber had landed guest spots on the television series "Get Smart," "Camp Runamuck," and "The Double Life of Henry Fife." After he introduced Del to the producers of the shows, Del made a few guest appearances on these shows and later became a character on the TV program that has been called the worst sitcom in the history of television, *My Mother the Car*. Del also starred along with several other members of The Committee in the counterculture film *Gold*. He played the part of "Che," a hippie prospector consumed by sex and drugs.

Del stayed with The Committee for four and a half years, becoming a leading figure in the anti-Establishment culture that raged in California. He had spent the decade drinking, smoking, shooting up, protesting, and having sex with any woman who would sleep with him. His hard living accelerated his inner demons. Thoughts of suicide increased, and his behavior became more erratic. Finally the West Coast ceased to excite him. In 1969 Chicago once again became his destination; he hitchhiked back.

Upon arrival he continued to experiment with the Harold. The work he had done in San Francisco wasn't finished, and the Chicago theater community rejuvenated him. He was obsessed with exploring all facets of long-form improvisation. So dedicated was he to the study of improv that he initially offered his workshops free of charge. He rented different studios and cafés so that he and his followers had a place to study and perform.

"We were like gypsies, traveling from one theater to the next. Those students were insanely devoted to this art form we were developing. That's when people started calling improv a cult," Del recalled.

People of all ages and from all walks of life performed at the different theaters and cafés that Del hired for his group's weekly performances. Eventually Del rented the Body Politic, where students like Betty Thomas performed the Harold in front of appreciative audiences. He named his company the Chicago Extension Improv Company. His collection of students began to increase to the point where Del was doing three and four classes a week.

When word got around town that Del was back, students and performers began asking him for personal workshops. Afraid that his already damaged relationship with Second City would be further deteriorated, he let the theater know that he hadn't sought out the performers, they had approached him. To his surprise, Second City thought the workshops were a good idea and encouraged Del to work further with its actors.

When Paul Sills gave Del a job performing in his Story Theater, Del returned to Los Angeles to perform at the Mark Taper Forum. Story Theater, a reworking of fairy tales mostly taken from the brothers Grimm, shut down after a few weeks. Del was cast for small parts in the forgettable *Son of the Blob* and *American Graffiti*—though there he felt he was a major part of the production. "None of the cast would have had any drugs without me," Del said. "I spent the entire filming of that movie getting everybody loaded."

After Paul Sills ended his show in Los Angeles, Del looked for a way back to Chicago. To his surprise, Second City came calling. The producers asked him to resume his teaching and directing for them. When he arrived, he was named the theater's resident director.

"I always valued Del for his ability and his intelligence, and I always felt he was rescuable," Bernie Sahlins said in hiring Del for a second time. Del was back at Second City.

30

The Sanctity of Marriage

It was hot and sticky. Not surprisingly, my truck didn't have air conditioning. The heat was unbearable.

The summer of 1998 was the hottest summer in Chicago since 1931. It wasn't unusual for temperatures to be in the upper nineties. The heat index often made the temperatures seem ten to fifteen degrees hotter. Luckily, Del had been showering each week before our visits.

Sweat was pouring down our faces as we returned from the bank. The Corrus Bank sign at Clark and Armitage flashed ninety-seven degrees on its digital display. It was mid-June and felt like it was actually getting hotter.

I was wearing a white cotton shirt underneath a Cubs baseball jersey. Del was wearing his usual dirty blue jeans, black T-shirt, and long-sleeve denim button-down. He always wore a long-sleeve shirt over his T-shirt to hide the track marks on his arms.

Del was leaning toward the window trying to take in as much breeze as possible. Sweat rolled down his forehead, collecting in his beard.

"So glad I bothered taking a shower this morning. What a total waste," Del grumbled as his beard continued to grow wet.

I looked at the gauges on the dashboard. The temperature needle was pushing toward the red line. If we weren't careful, we were going to overheat. We were still several blocks from Del's house, and the stop-and-go traffic really worried me. While Del was preoccupied, I flipped the heater on. Blowing the heat out of the engine and into the truck would keep us stable for a while.

As we drove along, I told Del I would have to miss the following week because I had to drive to central Illinois for a wedding. Del rolled his eyes and gave me advice as to what to get the couple as a gift.

"Tell them not to do it. That's the best gift you can give them."

I responded, "That's great advice from a lifelong bachelor."

The warm air from the engine was blowing through the heating vents, and Del's glasses kept sliding down his nose. "Shows what you know," he grunted. I wiped my head with the sleeve of my baseball jersey and looked at Del quizzically.

"I was married," he said nonchalantly.

"When?"

"While I was in California. During the sixties," he answered.

"That's the most vague thing I've ever heard," I said and laughed. "What happened?"

"We got married in a Buddhist ceremony. Then we realized a little while later that it was a mistake and got a divorce." He ran his hands through his hair, which molded to his head like he had just stepped out of a swimming pool.

"Who did you marry?" I asked him.

He shrugged and changed the subject. "I was engaged to a woman named Martha when I was in college also. So I've had a little more experience than you think, wise guy."

"What happened? Why didn't you marry her?" I asked.

"Martha was ten years older than me. I was still in college. She decided that getting married would ruin my life and there were better things for me, so she broke it off." He stared out the window.

"That's too bad," I told him. "You could have probably still carried on your career. Mike Nichols and all those Second City guys got married pretty young and it turned out all right."

He looked at me out of the corner of his eye and bit his lip.

"One morning she woke up, turned over, and told me it was over," he said and arched his eyebrows.

"Yikes," I responded.

"No fucking kidding. Two weeks later I went to her house and saw that she had packed everything up to leave. She broke it off and moved in with her parents. I never heard from her again."

We sat there quietly for a while, and I kept my eye on the temperature gauge. We were getting closer to his house. I kept a steady pace to try to avoid having to stop at any lights. When we passed Clark and Diversey without having to stop, it seemed like we were home free. I started to flip the heat off but thought better of it. Meanwhile, sweat patches were forming on Del's denim shirt. He was sweating through both of his shirts.

"Her name was Martha. What was the name of the woman you were married to?" I asked. He shook his head and took off his glasses. He tried to wipe the lenses, but only managed to smear sweat all over the frames.

"We were married less than two weeks."

I turned down Belmont and made our way toward Racine. We were in the clear, I reached up and flipped off the heat quickly when Del's head was turned, but he saw me out of the corner of his eye. He leaned in and inspected. "Did you have the fucking heat on?"

"What was your wife's name?" I asked, trying to change the subject.

"It's one hundred fucking degrees outside and you've got the goddamn heat on. What the hell is your problem?" Sweat dripped from his beard as he shook his head in amazement. "I've lost ten pounds in this fucking truck tonight," he announced.

We stopped in front of his house, and he got out. "It's cooler out here than it is in that lava pit of a car. I feel like a prisoner in the sweatbox at Alcatraz."

He wasn't so much angry as he was exasperated. I prodded him again to answer my question. "You still didn't tell me your wife's name."

"A tour of duty in the jungles of Vietnam would've been better than that heat trap you're driving around," he said and leaned through the window of the Ford.

I realized that there was a reason he hadn't answered my question. Otherwise he would have walked away and gone into his apartment.

"Why won't you tell me your wife's name?" If he didn't answer this time, I wouldn't ask him again.

Del pushed his sweat-streaked glasses up to the bridge of his nose. "The fact is, my dear friend, I can't tell you her name."

"Why?" I asked. He chewed on his lip as he stared at me through the window.

Unashamed, he answered, "I don't remember."

"What do you mean, you don't remember?"

"I didn't really know her too well before we got married, and then we were only married for a few days before we called it quits."

"You've got a marriage license and divorce papers, right?" I asked.

"I don't even remember where I put the *TV Guide* for this week. I've had to walk to the 7-11 three times this week to buy a new one," he answered.

I understood. I looked at him and said, "I bet if you thought about it or asked around, you'd be able to find out what her name was."

He stood away from the truck and smiled. "Why the hell would I want to do that?"

31

I-Beams and Columns

I had just shut the door and locked it on my way out when the phone rang inside my apartment. It was probably Del canceling or giving me last-minute instructions. I sighed and shuffled back inside to hear what he had to say this time.

"Bring your head-shot and resumé when you come," he ordered.

I couldn't imagine why he would possibly need those at the bank or the grocery store. I printed a resumé off my computer and stapled it to the back of my eight-by-ten picture. My resumé was pretty bare. I had my recent improv experience on it, but the rest of the listings were college credits. I tried to disguise them to look like I had performed in Chicago, but I wasn't about to fool anyone.

"We're going to my agent's office today. I think you should give her your head shot when we get up there," Del announced as he climbed into the truck.

"I'm not really dressed for that Del," I said with some concern in my voice. It was a pleasant spring day. I was wearing denim shorts and an old Cubs baseball jersey.

"Don't worry about it," Del assured me. "I mean, look at me. I didn't dress up today."

He hadn't. And if they were willing to represent a homeless junkie, maybe they'd be willing to add on a punk kid who looked like he was headed out to the playground. But I was still a little worried. Actors were told they should always present themselves to an agent in the best possible manner. Dress up, look nice, put on a show.

Del set down his head shots on the seat between us and picked up mine.

"Very nice," he mumbled.

"You think?"

"Oh yes," he nodded. "I was worried that you would have a fake, commercial-friendly picture. Everybody usually looks so fucking phony and plastic in their shots."

"These aren't like that?" I was looking for a little assurance.

"Not at all. They capture your personality perfectly. You look like a real dickhead here," he said, thinking he was giving me a compliment. He stared at the picture for a while and then added, "God, you look like an asshole in this picture. Who did these?"

"Suzanne Plunkett."

"She did mine too," he said excitedly. "Wouldn't it be funny if Elizabeth Geddes became your agent? We'd have the same photographer and agent."

I looked at him suspiciously. He sounded like he was in grade school. He was being pretty genuine.

The Geddes Agency occupied offices on the top floor of the four-floor Royal George Theater building. The upper floors contained offices for a variety of businesses; the first floor housed three theater spaces. *Forever Plaid* had played in the dinner theater area for years while the other two performance stages rotated productions pretty frequently.

Del and I walked through the lobby of the theater complex and headed toward the corridor that contained the elevator. The lobby was lavishly decorated and brightly lit. Light boxes show-cased the different productions currently playing in the theaters.

As we turned the corner to enter the corridor that led to the elevator, it took a few seconds for our eyes to adjust. It was quite a contrast to the ornately decorated section we were leaving; it looked rather dark and starkly adorned. All the woodwork was exposed to give it the look and feel of a mountainside Swiss chalet. A wooden column extended from ceiling to floor for no apparent reason. A thick, solid beam protruded horizontally from the column and jutted out two feet into the walkway area.

For the life of me, I couldn't understand why the beam was there. It was three feet high and served no architectural pur-pose. As we walked through the dim hall, I wondered to myself why the beam extended so far from the wall.

Del wasn't paying attention to his surroundings because he was excitedly talking about the good news he had received about some of his former students. The Upright Citizens Brigade was a group that had started in Chicago, moved to New York, and opened their own theater. They had received word that Comedy Central wanted them to put together a weekly half-hour piece to follow "South Park." Del was ecstatic.

I waited for Del to stop talking about the UCB so I could point out the obstructive wood beam. But he kept talking and walking—right into the beam.

"Goosh" was the sound he made as his stomach slammed into the thick piece of wood.

He doubled over and grabbed his belly. "What the fuck was that?"

I clenched my teeth to keep from laughing and tried to sound attentive and concerned, "Are you okay?"

He remained bent over and let out a big breath, "Yeah. It hit me in the gut."

A small chuckle escaped, and my eyes started to water. I looked away and tried to look angry. I couldn't look at him because the sight of him standing there with his hands on his big belly was so funny.

"You hit that so hard, Del," I said, choking back a laugh.

"It's so fucking dark in here, I never saw it coming. It was like someone sneaked up and slapped me in the gut with a two-by-four," he said as he turned to look at the beam.

"It's way too dark in here," I agreed. "It's so bright in the other hallway, you feel like you're walking into a cave when you come in here."

He coughed a bit and straightened up. He opened his eyes wide and exclaimed, "Jesus Christ, that hurt!"

"You never broke stride. You walked into it full speed like it was some cartoon." I chuckled. I had gained enough composure to let out a laugh without it developing into an all-out roar.

"Why did you let me walk into it like a jackass if you saw I was going toward it?" he asked as we walked to the elevator. I couldn't look at him. Every time I did, I pictured him slapping into the beam and the shock on his face.

"I didn't think there was any way you didn't see it," I said, trying to excuse myself.

"I'd like to go one day without you trying to kill me," he growled as we stepped into the creaky old elevator.

"Del, I was waiting for you to stop talking so I could tell you to watch out for the stupid beam. I didn't want to interrupt you," I said apologetically.

"Next time warn me before I hit the beam, you fucking twit. I don't mind being interrupted if I'm about to do bodily harm to myself." We stood and waited for the elevator to arrive at the fourth floor. Del slid his hand up and rubbed his belly.

I tried to think of something else, but my mind was zoned in on one image. Finally I let it out, "You said 'Goosh' when you slapped into the beam." Tears rolled down my cheeks, and I couldn't hold the laughter back any longer.

"I hit that thing so goddamn hard." Del started laughing himself.

As we walked into the agent's office, Del couldn't stop giggling. He introduced me to Elizabeth Geddes, and the three of us discussed my previous experience. Del made some flattering comments about my talents as an improviser, but you could tell she was suspicious because he and I twittered at everything he said.

He assured her that neither of us was under any substance. Our jubilant mood was a result of his narrow escape from a recent assassination attempt. Thoroughly confused, Elizabeth scheduled an audition for me to perform a monologue for her and her associates.

Elizabeth offered us some cookies that one of her clients had given her. Del started laughing again as I talked to her, causing him to spit out crumbs that landed on his beard. We left the office but didn't settle down until we stepped back into the elevator. We stood silently as we regained our composure and waited to arrive at the first floor.

"That was terribly inappropriate," Del exhaled as the doors opened and we walked back into the corridor of doom. "I'm very fond of Elizabeth. I hope she doesn't think I'm some giggling ninny now."

As we passed by the column, I pointed to the beam and said, "Watch out for the beam, Grandpa."

"Fuck off, retard."

32

Hurt Feelings

The Chicago Improv Festival had produced a symposium during its weeklong festivities and invited several leaders of the Chicago improv community to speak to the students and answer their questions. Mick Napier from the Annoyance Theatre and Del were invited to be part of it while Martin DeMaat represented Second City.

Martin was the artistic director for the Second City Training Center. He and Del hated each other. I had taken a couple of classes with Martin when I first arrived in Chicago; he had made a few disparaging comments about Del and Improv-Olympic during our class time.

In the middle of our scenes, Martin had stopped us to give notes. He finished by telling us, "You can completely ignore my notes if you want. I'm not a deranged crackpot drug abuser that has been falsely elevated to deity status. My thoughts on improv don't matter, I guess."

He had continued giving notes, and when he was finished he turned to us as if he were telling us a secret and said, "I was talking about Del Close, by the way. Awful man. Terrible man."

That was the first time I had heard Del Close's name mentioned. I never told Del about those comments because he really didn't need more fuel to keep that fire toward Martin burning.

The panel discussion for the festival was taking place in the early afternoon at Second City. I met Del immediately afterward so that we could run our errands. I arrived at his apartment early and sat in the truck to wait for him. He was running late, so I ran into the hardware store and bought some clear plastic and duck tape.

Charna pulled up and dropped Del off as I walked out of the store. She had her convertible top down, and I could hear Del yelling in the car. I grimaced as his voice grew angrier and louder. I didn't want to deal with him if he was in a bad mood.

He walked over to the truck and barked that he was ready to go.

"You all right?" I asked as we headed downtown toward the bank.

"That fucking faggot sabotaged the whole thing," he yelled. He wasn't so much angry as he was exasperated and disappointed.

According to Del, the panel discussion had deteriorated into a snipping fight between Del and Martin. Del had tried to make a point about long-form improv and how ImprovOlympic focused all its energy on teaching slow, organic scene work. Martin had interrupted him and commented that the symposium wasn't supposed to be a commercial for the different theaters. Del told me that he had let the interruption go the first time. When it happened again, he snapped back and told Martin to stop interrupting him. After that, it was on. Throughout the symposium, the two of them battled back and forth while Mick sat in the middle looking composed, intelligent, and witty.

"It was embarrassing," Del sighed. "I just don't understand why it had to sink to this. I was trying not to get into it with him, but he wouldn't stop and he was getting very personal with his comments, so I had to shoot back to defend myself and Charna. We looked like idiots up there."

The improv community had always said that if Del was the stern father figure of improv, Martin was the warm, supportive mother. Very few people had ever heard a harsh word from Martin. Because of that, it was surprising to see how obstinate he could be with Del.

"I don't know what I did to that fairy to make him treat me like that."

I knew this wasn't the appropriate time to question his use of language, but I couldn't stop myself.

"Maybe he treats you like that because you call him things like 'fag' and 'fairy.'" I was stepping straight into a fight.

"What the hell am I supposed to call him then?" he barked at me so loud that it surprised and scared me. "If it bothers him so much that I call him names, he should go 'give himself a hug,'" Del said, mocking Martin's trademark phrase.

"You could call him the teacher from Second City, the artistic director of the training center of Second City, or you could make it a lot easier and call him Marty or Martin or Mr. De-Maat. . . ."

"I'd rather fucking die. Why are you taking his side?"

I was getting unnerved and wished I hadn't invited this argument. "I'm not defending what happened today. I'm just saying that you dilute your argument when you resort to calling him a fairy. It's just immature and childish," I said, with all the composure I could muster.

"I think interrupting me and mocking my comments is immature," he rebutted loudly.

"You're right. I think you're probably right about the whole issue. You're just not going to get any sympathy when you call him names like that."

"Take me home," he commanded. "I'm sick of this shit."

"Del," I reasoned with him, "if he interrupted you and mocked you, he was wrong."

I didn't get the rest of the sentence out because Del started screaming at me. "'If!' 'If!' 'If'," he shouted. I just *told* you that he did. Why are you questioning that it happened any different than what I told you?" I turned the truck home.

There was no way I was continuing this trip. I'd made him very angry, and there was no fixing it.

"You always do this," he shouted at me. "You always take everyone else's side!"

"I'm not taking his side. I'm just saying that he's probably at home upset about the whole situation too. He probably doesn't think that he was doing any harm."

"He blatantly tried to humiliate me!" Del screamed at me so loud that I instinctively slapped my hand to my ear.

I pulled up in front of his house, and he opened the door. "I'm sorry you were embarrassed today, Del. I didn't mean to make you angrier."

"Well, you failed miserably, fuckhead," he yelled as he slammed the door.

I stepped out of the truck and shouted more apologies at Del as he walked toward the gate that led to his doorway. "Del, don't be mad. I'm sorry."

He kept walking and raised his hand in the air as he opened the gate and disappeared from view.

I had just managed to accelerate a large flame into an all-out bonfire.

33

Wastelands

Del called to tell me he was feeling a little depressed and asked if I would go to the movies with him.

I picked him up on the way to the Webster theater. I was surprised to hear that the movie Del wanted to see was *The Faculty*. Every few years Hollywood falls into a teen-slasher movie craze; *The Faculty* was their latest creation. Del was always in the mood to see a horror movie. It seemed like just the type of thing to cheer him up.

We loaded up on concessions and took our seats. We were early so we talked while we waited for the movie to start. Del's booming voice echoed through the theater, so everyone was privy to our conversation.

Del got hungry for Junior Mints and sent me to the concessions counter. When I returned I saw two long-haired guys in black T-shirts talking to Del. They looked like they were talking to an ethereal being. They kept giggling and elbowing each other every time Del spoke. As I approached, I understood who they were. They were fans.

One of the guys took off running as I walked down the row to my seat.

"Where's he going?" Del asked Fan Number Two.

"He thinks he has one of your graphic novels in his car," the fan said.

They were admirers of Del's comic book. They hadn't looked or acted like the fans who usually recognized Del.

The two of them continued to talk. I tried to appear interested, but they may as well have been speaking Russian. I knew little about comic books, and they were engrossed in a pretty intense discussion.

Fan Number One came galloping down the aisle and slid next to his friend. He handed a copy of *Wasteland* to Del. "Hoo, hoo, hoo," Del cackled. "Lookie here."

He took a pen from Fan Number One and signed his autograph on the first page inside the cover. The two men continued to gush over Del, and I leaned forward and looked at the small book in Del's hand.

"That's your comic book?" I asked Del.

"You've never seen it?"

I shrugged, and Del looked at his two new friends. They were aghast that I was sitting next to this man they considered a legendary genius, and I'd never witnessed his work.

"Can my little retarded friend look at your book?" Del asked Fan Number One.

I flipped through the book and saw all the gruesome images it contained. It was a horror series. Del and his co-writer John Ostrander had written the books to be psychologically frightening as well as violently intimidating.

The lights flickered, the previews began. I handed the comic book to Del who gave it back to his two fans. They shook his hand and took their seats several rows behind us. I looked at Del and smiled, but he continued to stare straight ahead.

"What are you smiling at?" he asked me.

"There's no way you can still be depressed after that. You made their day."

I stared at him until finally he turned to me and smiled and said, "Stop fucking looking at me."

After the movie I drove to Del's apartment. He ordered me to come inside for a few minutes, and then he disappeared into his front room. I sat down at the table and waited for him to return. He walked back into the kitchen and slapped a stack of comic books in front of me. I looked at the cover of one and grimaced. It was *Wasteland*, issue number one. The cover featured a marriage between two ghouls surrounded by wailing skeletons.

"I want you to read a few of these and then take the rest home and read them," he told me. He picked up the copy on top of the stack and began to read it.

The first issue portrayed Del roller-skating through the sewers of Chicago with a butane torch strapped to his head while shooting rats with a BB gun. "This says that this sewer story is autobiographical. Is that true?" I asked.

"Yes," Del answered. He seemed offended that I had questioned the authenticity of the story.

I read a few more and asked Del to clarify the reality of the other stories. He verified their validity and told me about some of the story lines that had been rejected. They were pretty offensive.

"It's hard to imagine you being like you were in these stories," I told him.

"I was a bit wilder in my younger days," he admitted. We both knew that was a gross understatement.

"If we'd met twenty years ago, I don't think we would have liked each other very much," I told him.

He agreed. "We would have hated each other. I think we would have performed well together, but you're a little too strait-laced and squeaky clean for my tastes back then."

"Yeah," I sighed. "I'm pretty sure I would have hated you."

"I would have thought you were a narc, a fag, or an asshole," Del said. I gathered the comic books and put them in an envelope.

"It's interesting how a difference of twenty short years can affect a relationship," Del commented. "We would have missed out on a pretty good friendship."

I looked at the scraggly old man who stood across the table from me. He was only sixty-three, but looked fifteen years older. His beard was white as snow, and his overly large glasses were so smudged I wondered how he could see out of them. He was a physically large man, but he seemed small and lonely in front of me.

"You're a good friend, Del," I told him.

"Thank you. Thanks for going to the movies this afternoon," he said.

I put the envelope of comic books on the table and sat back down. "You want to order a pizza and read the rest of your comic books?"

"Can I get high when we're done eating?" Del asked.

I rolled my eyes. "I don't care. Just remember to say goodbye when I leave."

As Del read *Wasteland*. I called and ordered a pepperoni and green olive pizza from Giordano's. Del explained all the story lines and dictated the complete process of putting together a graphic novel. After we ate pizza, Del smoked some pot. The stories about his comic book tales became a little wilder and a bit unbelievable.

I finished the final edition and looked up to see that Del had fallen asleep in his chair. I put the copies of *Wasteland* in the envelope and left a note on his refrigerator.

I slipped out of the apartment and headed home. An awfully nice day had turned into a pretty great evening.

34

Old Companions with Pictures

He was distracted. I had mistakenly thought he was depressed.

I drove by a bookstore twice to try to cheer him up, but he didn't even notice. His mind was on something else. I drove back around and pointed at the book hole, but he shrugged his shoulders and murmured that he'd rather go home.

I was floored. I took him home and carried his cat food and groceries up to the apartment.

Del poured a cup of tea for me but neglected to pour one for himself. He sat down with his elbow on the table and put his chin in his hand. The mug of tea was usually produced before we left to run our errands. The fact that he set it on the table now meant that he wanted something else from me.

I sat at the table and ignored the tea. I looked at him for a few moments as he stared off into the distance. We sat there for a while until Del picked up an envelope and pulled out a photo. He looked at it for a few minutes and then handed it to me.

It was a picture of a curly-haired man standing in the middle of a brightly decorated kitchen. There was a vague familiarity to the man.

"Who does he look like?" Del asked as I investigated the picture more closely.

"It looks like you," I answered him.

I set the picture down and Del quietly picked it up. He sighed as he looked at the photo.

"It's not me," he muttered vacantly.

"It's not you? I thought it was an old picture of you."

"I don't think it looks like me," he said as he studied it intently.

"The nose. The eyes. The pretentious smile. It totally looks like you," I told him.

He put the photo back in the envelope and set it aside. "What does it matter?" He put his chin back in his palm and stared off again.

"Who's the picture of?" I asked. He heard the question but didn't respond. He looked at me and looked away again.

With his glance, I understood everything. We sat there until I broke the silence.

"Is that your son, Del?" I quietly asked.

He nodded and continued to stare off. I reached across the table, took the picture out of the envelope, and looked at it again. There was no doubt that this was indeed Del's son.

"Do you really think he looks like me?" Del asked as he continued to stare off into space.

"I do," I told him. "Where did you get the picture?"

"His mother read an article about me in a magazine and wrote to ask if I was the same Del Close who had been involved with her thirty-five years ago. I wrote her back and gave her my phone number, and she called a couple of weeks ago."

He didn't look at me once while he was telling the story. I couldn't read his emotions. He didn't seem to be sad or regretful. He just seemed enigmatic.

On one of Del's many trips to various mental institutions, he met a nurse who became enamored with his spirit and intellect. Shortly before he was due to be discharged, she went to him, begging him to help her conceive a child. She promised Del that he would have no responsibility, she just wanted to have a child that carried his genes.

Del knew his son was out there, but he hadn't heard from the nurse in decades. Charna had begged him to try to get in touch with the woman and his son, but Del simply responded, "I can't get emotional about a forty-year-old man with hairy arms."

Del busied himself playing with the keychain I had bought him for his birthday. I watched to see if I could read any emotion from him.

"She asked if she could send me pictures of our son." He paused before he added, "I shouldn't have said yes."

"Why?"

"Because I keep looking at it," he answered.

He looked at me, and I took the picture out again. A second picture fell out with it. The same curly-haired man stood in the same brightly decorated kitchen. In this picture though, he was not alone. He held in his arms an infant boy. I raised my eyebrows and looked up at Del.

"I'd like to introduce you to my grandson," Del announced as I handed him both pictures.

"Wow, Del. Pretty heavy," I said.

He put the pictures back in the envelope and handed it to me. "Take these with you please. I have no emotion for either of them, but I can't get past the curiosity of it all. I keep letting my mind wander," Del said as he stood and poured himself some tea.

"Del," I started, but he interrupted.

"It's all right. It's all very intriguing, but it will just lead me down a road that never existed. And roads like that lead to nowhere but trouble." Del sipped his tea and turned on the television.

I took the envelope and made my way back to my apartment. Once inside, I heard Del's baritone rumble on my voice mail.

"Don't throw those pictures away," he said, exhaling deeply. "I imagine there's a chance I might ask for them back."

He never did.

35

Note Taken

My Harold improv team, Monkey Rocket, was disman-
tled, and I was reassigned to a new team named Deep Schwa.
Deep Schwa was made up of veterans and was classified as a
mid-level team. There were four categories of teams at Improv-
Olympic: house teams, mid-level teams, probationary teams,
and new teams (in descending order). All the teams worked
hard to become house teams, the groups that performed on Friday and Saturday nights and usually closed out the show on
other nights.

Spoo, my performance class that Del had directed, was now
performing on Saturdays at 10:30 p.m. with the Lindbergh Babies. We weren't as polished and celebrated as the Lindbergh
Babies, but we put on an entertaining show every week. Del
liked us enough that he kept the two shows paired together permanently.

Having Del as a director was like having my father as my
Little League coach. He would heap loads of praise on me for
the positive things I would do while the rest of the class whispered comments about my being the teacher's pet. Conversely,
any mistake I made was met with a wrath and ire that no one
else received.

In our fourth show I had spent an entire scene talking about a character who wasn't on stage. The invisible person became more important than my partner in the scene. Del was livid. Except for that scene, I had done well. Our whole team felt pretty good about the entire evening because the show had been great. Del could care less.

Backstage after the show, he ripped into me. "You have a scene partner on stage with you. Why in the hell would you waste their time and ours talking about a person that to this point doesn't exist?"

I stood in the center of the room and took my lumps as everyone listened to Del launch into a tirade.

"There's another person on stage. Use them. By discussing a person that's not onstage with you, you are negating your relationship with your scene partner and destroying the continuity of the world that is being established on stage."

My teammates were becoming uncomfortable. None of them would look in my direction.

"Maybe you would just rather have no one do scenes with you so that you can do all your scenes by yourself and invent all your scene partners. The two of you are there to deal with each other—why the hell would you invent someone we can't see? You're in a scene with another person—talk to them, not about other people."

He was finished and I was expected to respond. There was only one thing to say: "Note taken."

Del nodded, and everyone left to go his or her separate way. They shuffled out and left me standing alone. I walked out of the theater wondering if Del would be waiting. He wasn't. His tirade was never mentioned again.

36

Second City—Again

When Del came back to Chicago in 1972, the Second City cast included Brian Doyle-Murray, Harold Ramis, Martin De-Maat, Joe Flaherty, and a wild young man named John Belushi.

Del's work with The Committee had won him a reputation that impressed cast members and audiences alike. His study of improv as an art form now influenced his directing. He began to push the idea of "group mind." Instead of allowing players to get caught up in their solo performances, he urged them to perform as a collective existence. As the structure that had been established in earlier Second City productions was relaxed, Del pushed the performers to take bigger chances and explore emotions and ideas that they otherwise would have suppressed.

Del wrote and directed a classic scene on a subject that would normally have been considered taboo: death. The scene involved a funeral in which mourners suppressed their amusement over the death of a friend who had met his demise after getting his head stuck in a can of Van Camp's beans.

Influenced by his highly political Committee days, Del also promoted scenes that satirized local and national government. Second City had always lampooned individual politicians, but

under Del's direction the shows began to challenge and de-
nounce government and big business. Mayor Richard J. Daley
and Richard Nixon became frequent targets as Del's rebellious
nature influenced the cast. It was essential, he thought, for this
satirical company to have a strong voice of social commentary.

John Belushi was often the man tapped to play Mayor Daley. Del was intrigued by Belushi's wild and uncontrollable
personality and attracted to his talent. He had found a protégé
in his own mold. He took Belushi under his wing and spent
hours with him discussing acting, comedy, and improv. The two
men struggled with Del's constant urging for Belushi to play at
the height of his intelligence. The easy joke is always there,
Del would explain, but the performer must resist it and try to
entertain the audience cerebrally.

Comedy wasn't the only thing the two men shared. Both of
them were frequent drug users, and Del introduced John to
drugs that he never knew existed. Del lived across the street
from Second City then, and the two of them would smoke marijuana before the show and shoot heroin afterward.

John Belushi's career skyrocketed when he left Second City
at the end of 1972 to join National Lampoon's production of
"Lemmings." In 1975 he auditioned for a late-night sketch
show that was to debut on NBC, called "Saturday Night Live."
The first image of the show broadcast was that of Belushi learning English by repeating the words, "I'd like to feed your fin-
gertips to wolverines." He stayed on the show for four years and
filmed *Animal House* and Steven Spielberg's *1941* during that
time. After he left the show that made him famous, his popu-
larity rose further with the production of *The Blues Brothers*,
with his fellow Second City alum Dan Aykroyd.

Belushi returned to Chicago often to visit his family and
would stop by Del's apartment on each visit. Del would coun-

sel John on his career, and the two of them would then spend the rest of the visit shooting each other up with drugs John had brought from New York and California.

Second City knew of Del's drug usage but felt he was in good shape and was controlling his addictions. When the company decided to open a theater in Toronto, Del traveled there to help choose the cast that would perform in a 250-seat cabaret on Adelaide Street, with the backing of Andrew Alexander.

It was at these auditions that Del and Bernie Sahlins discovered John Candy, Gilda Radner, and Dan Aykroyd. Del liked Candy so much that he brought him to Chicago to join a cast that now included Bill Murray, Ann Ryerson, and Betty Thomas.

George Wendt and Shelley Long would be elevated by Del in the coming years, as would Eugene Levy, Dave Thomas, Martin Short, and John Belushi's brother Jim. Del's appraisal of talent was unmatched; he discovered brilliant performers, then cultivated and refined their skills. Producers and agents began traveling to Chicago to steal away Second City actors at an alarming rate.

Realizing their talent was being snatched for the riches of "Saturday Night Live" and other television programs, Second City decided to develop its own TV show. Bernie Sahlins and Del met with Andrew Alexander and the Second City Toronto cast and agreed on a concept for a weekly series. SCTV would be the call letters for a fictional television network that was so impoverished it had to cram its entire day's programming into a half-hour segment. Second City would satirize the media and especially television with spoofs of contemporary TV fare. The show ran for 7 years and 185 episodes, was nominated for 13 Emmys, and received 2 for writing.

"SCTV" introduced the world to John Candy, Eugene Levy, Martin Short, Catherine O'Hara, Dave Thomas, Rick Moranis, and Joe Flaherty. The importance of Del's contribution to the show was immeasurable.

But as successful as he was, Del couldn't overcome his feelings of inadequacy. His drinking increased to the point that in 1978 he and Severn Darden checked themselves into the Schick Shadel Hospital in Fort Worth, Texas, for radical aversion therapy. Del described the experience to *Chicago* magazine: "They dry you out for three days, give you a little booze so you don't go into hideous withdrawal. And then they shoot you up with these chemicals. It makes you violently, violently ill—intergalactic nausea. Nobody on earth has ever been that sick. Then you drink highly diluted, warm, and slightly salted versions of whatever drink you like, and ooh, you throw up for about an hour and a half. They then put you in a bed and give you sodium pentothal. Which gets you whacked; this is the reward part of the therapy. It also could be used as a hypnotic; they can sneak past the censor by giving you posthypnotic suggestions. So they come at you every which way."

While the treatment cured Del of his addiction to alcohol, his abuse of drugs continued. Del and Severn Darden developed a fondness for plastizone, a drug that slowed the heart and produced a drifting, floating feeling. They also were attached to chemical mescaline, a solvent used in developing film. And heroin, cocaine, and valium were consistent recreational distractions.

During this second stint with Second City, Del often ended up in a sanitarium as his suicide attempts became more frequent. The responsibility for picking Del up and getting him to the theater was rotated among the cast members. Each time Del was institutionalized, producers would send a cleaning crew from the theater to do a thorough sweep of his apartment. Tales of deteriorating food, feces on the floor, and cockroaches raining from the ceiling were legendary and all too believable.

Jim Belushi once approached Del at the theater during one of Del's dark periods. He told Del, "I know you're having problems, and I know that everyone's mad at you here and you're alone. I just want you to know that I love you and trust you."

Del asked Jim, "You trust me?"

Jim responded, "Yeah, Del, I do. You've done a lot for me. I really trust you."

Enthusiastically, Del asked again, "You trust me?"

"Yeah," Jim reassured him.

With that, Del reared back and kicked Jim squarely in the groin.

While Del's professional career had reached new heights, his emotional and mental states were morbid. He could spend an entire day doing brilliant work, then spend the evening laughing and conversing with friends. Soon he'd excuse himself for a few moments. Sirens would fill the air, and everyone would look around and notice that Del hadn't returned. They knew why the ambulance had arrived.

He was tortured. When asked about the cause of his torture, he would reply simply, "Everything."

37

Sweet and Sour Pork

Del went through phases with his dietary habits. When he liked a type of food, he'd stay faithful to it until he got bored and decided to move to something else. In the summer of 1998 he was obsessed with Mexican food.

We traveled all over the city looking for restaurants to satisfy his craving. One of his students told Del about a place in Bridgeport that supposedly had the best Mexican sweet and sour pork in the city. On a sweltering afternoon, Del and I jumped in my truck and drove to the South Side for some south-of-the-border delicacies.

We parked behind the three-story building located southwest of Forty-first and Halsted. From the outside the place looked dirty and deserted. It didn't look much better on the inside.

There were three tables and a large white counter. Behind the counter, a lighted sign listed the items that were on the menu—no prices.

"How do we know how much everything costs?" I asked Del as we sat at one of the tables.

"I don't know," he said. "But I can't wait to find out."

A short Hispanic man suddenly appeared and asked us what we wanted to eat. Del ordered sweet and sour pork for each of us. The man nodded and asked that we pay him immediately. This amused Del greatly, and he reached for his wallet. The waiter initially told us that the two meals would cost us eight dollars, but he changed his mind when Del attempted to hand him the money. He had made a mistake, he said. The cost of the food was now seven dollars. When Del inquired as to why the price had changed, the waiter told us that Del's meal cost four dollars and mine cost three.

We were utterly confused. We had ordered the exact same thing.

As we waited for our food to arrive, I pointed out to Del that there were eleven chairs for the three tables, and no two chairs were alike.

My food arrived first; Del's arrived five minutes later. I waited for his to come before I began eating.

The first bite told me something was wrong. It was cold. And mushy. The first bite had rice and beans with the pork. I figured those things had caused the cold, mushy taste in my mouth.

The second bite was fine. I listened to Del talk about the "X-Files" episode he had seen the previous evening. Then I ran into a cold squish again with the next forkful of food.

"Is your food all right?" I asked Del. He was annoyed that I had interrupted his story, but he stabbed at my food and tasted it for himself.

"It's fine. What's your problem?" he answered gruffly.

He continued with his story as I tried another bite—but this one led to my undoing. I bit into the pork and felt blood squirt through my mouth. I gagged, and Del looked up startled.

"Are you going to barf?" he asked with concern. I couldn't answer because I was afraid that if I opened my mouth, vomit would hurtle out.

Del took another bite of my food and spat it out in his napkin. "This is raw." He took my plate and inspected it closer. "Half of this is cooked and half of it's raw. I see why your meal was a dollar less."

My stomach gurgled. Del yelled into the kitchen for the location of the bathroom. There wasn't one. The waiter told us to go into the alley.

I inhaled deeply through my nose and tried to get control of my gag reflex. Del motioned that we should leave but started hurriedly shoveling food into his mouth. I stood up and walked a few feet to the door. Del crammed as much food as he could into his mouth and followed me out. We turned the corner and heard a crash as we headed toward the rear of the building.

Two twelve-year-old boys were running from the parking lot. One of them held a tire iron and the other carried a small white paper bag. They ran in two separate directions and disappeared within seconds.

Del hurried as quickly as he could to the truck, but we both knew what the boys had run off with. He arrived at the truck and put his hands on his head in disbelief.

He yelled at me, "Go get them! They broke the window and took all my medicine."

We had stopped at Walgreens to pick up Del's prescriptions before going to eat.

I took two steps to run after the boys and stopped dead in my tracks. I put my hand over my mouth, but it didn't help. Everything was coming back up, and my hand wasn't going to keep it in. Vomit exploded from my stomach and spurted everywhere as I fell to my knees. I could feel the glass from my broken window cutting into my knees.

"Jesus Christ," Del muttered. "What a mess."

He walked back into the Mexican restaurant and came back with a towel. "They didn't even have napkins," he griped. "I told them they served you raw food and gave you food poisoning, but they're saying it couldn't have been their food."

I wiped my face and hands and stood up. Blood trickled down my knees, and I used a clean part of the towel to try to wipe it off. Del took the towel and dipped it into my vomit. After he felt it was appropriately soaked, he walked to the front of the restaurant and threw it against the glass storefront. He hurried to the truck and swept away the broken glass in the seat.

"What did you do?" I asked as I heard yelling from inside the restaurant.

"Chicago retribution," he cackled and admonished me to get the truck started.

I backed the truck out of the parking lot and drove away, fast. The workers in the restaurant screamed obscenities at us as we raced away. Not to be outdone, Del leaned out the window and shouted a steady stream of off-color epithets.

Instead of heading back toward the North Side, I turned and drove in the direction of the boys who had stolen Del's medicine. "Don't worry about it," Del said as we drove around looking for two pre-teens. "I'll call my doctor and tell him what happened, and we'll get a refill later."

I pulled over into an alley and vomited again in a garbage can. Del took my ice scraper and used it to brush out as much glass as he could.

"I'm sorry," I groveled.

"What are you talking about? This is the most fun I've had in one day in a long time," he said with a mischievous glint in his eye.

On the way back to Del's place I stopped one more time to throw up. Along the way he told me about the time he met up with some unruly Bulls fans moments after the Bulls beat the Lakers in the NBA finals a few years back. He had been wearing a T-shirt that had "L.A." emblazoned across the front of it. The men came out of a convenience store and mistook Del for a Lakers fan. He kept trying to tell them that he was a Bulls fan, but they wouldn't listen. They turned him upside down and stuffed him in a garbage can.

I dropped him off in front of his apartment, and he thanked me for a fantastic day. It began to rain as I drove home. With the window busted out, the passenger seat was soaked.

I stepped into my apartment and headed straight to the bathroom to puke. I stepped into the shower, cleaned all the blood and vomit off my body, put on some fresh clothes, and crawled into bed.

I stayed there for three days.

38

Regrets

"What do you regret?" Del asked as we sat at a table eating lunch.

The question surprised me. It had come out of the blue, and I couldn't see where it originated. "I don't know. Why?"

"I look at you and I wonder if a strapping, young small-town boy like yourself wishes that he'd done anything different in his life," he responded.

"I guess," I said as I swirled my pancakes through some syrup. "Everybody makes mistakes."

"Like what," Del prodded.

I sighed and realized I wasn't going to escape without him extracting some information from me. "There's a young woman in Goodfield that I probably could have been married to if I'd been smarter. I guess I regret that. I have an old friend that I grew up with who can't open his mouth without telling a lie, and I wish I hadn't ignored that. I knew he was lying and stealing from me, but I ignored it because I didn't want to lose a friend. I regret that I didn't launch him as a friend earlier."

"Does it make you feel better to say those things?" he asked.

"A little," I answered. "Why are you obsessed with things that I regret?"

He set his fork down, chewing his lip. "I have an awful lot of regrets, my dear boy, and I wondered if that was normal."

I continued eating and tried to continue as if we were having a routine discussion. "It's normal. We all make mistakes. It's natural to think about them. What do you regret?" I asked.

He took a deep breath and exhaled. "I regret that I allowed years to go by without speaking to my mother. It hurt her, and I'm sorry that I caused her pain. I wish that I'd been a better friend to Jamie Swise and countless others who were loyal and dedicated to me. I wish I'd never touched a drop of alcohol because it fucked me up far worse than any of the fucking drugs I crammed into my body. I wish I hadn't messed up so badly in 1965 that Second City fired me. I went on to work with The Committee and that was astronomically important, but I regret that I was asked to leave a job I loved so much."

He continued eating as he listed all of his regrets. He did it so casually that I knew this was a list he had memorized. "I wish I had grabbed John Belushi and Chris Farley and shaken the life back into them when I saw they were out of control. I regret that I never asked my father if there was something wrong when I saw the pain in his eyes. I wish I had been patient enough to get a degree from one of the silly colleges I attended. It always made me feel so inadequate when I was with Severn.

"I wish I felt comfortable enough to call up Elaine and shoot the shit with her. I love that woman and respect the hell out of her, but she intimidates the hell out of me. I regret that I hated Mike Nichols so much. He was everyone's 'ideal man,' and I hated him for that because it was something I could never be. I wish I hadn't caused so many people to be fired. Those people didn't deserve to have their lives affected by me. I wish that now that I'm sixty-three years old, I didn't have the body of a ninety-year-old man.

"I just generally wish that I'd been a better friend, lover, and teacher to a great many people," he said.

I wanted to tell him that he'd done a lot of good over the years, that he was wasting his time thinking about his regrets. I decided not to. He didn't need me to tell him.

39

Tank Tops and Badgers

The gas tank was full and the windows were down as Del and I sped up I-94 on our way to Madison, Wisconsin. It was a beautiful Saturday morning, the temperature a comfortable eighty degrees.

Del had called me the previous Wednesday and asked if I wanted to make two hundred dollars. He needed someone to drive him to Madison so he could teach a workshop. He suggested that I call in sick from my tour-guide job to drive him there. It would be a full day's trip as we had to be at one of the theaters at the University of Wisconsin by noon. The daylong workshop culminated with a performance at eight Saturday evening. Most likely we wouldn't be headed back to Chicago until after midnight.

With the windows down and the wind whipping around, it was impossible to talk. About twenty minutes into the trip, Del fell asleep and didn't wake up until we pulled into Madison. We stopped for gas midway, but he didn't even rustle.

The red and white colors of the Wisconsin Badgers were everywhere in Madison. We found our way to the campus, and I maneuvered the truck toward the theater.

As we inched closer to our destination, Del prepared me for what was to occur throughout the day. "It's thirty college students, and they're going to be very tight and nervous. They're going to come flying out of the gates with all of their favorite wacky characters, and it's going to take me a couple of hours to beat it out of them. It's going to take some patience because they're going to treat the day like an audition instead of a workshop."

I asked Del whom he was running the workshops for, but he didn't know. He had originally thought it was for the university, but the people had called the night before and informed Del they were a private improv group that was renting out the theater.

"The key to teaching new students or students that have been taught incorrectly is to remain composed. Hostility and impatience only serve to stunt their growth. We have to realize that our mission today is not to erect the pyramid but to set up a solid foundation so that the construction can be completed effortlessly after we depart," Del told me as I rested the old truck into a parking spot.

A short, stocky guy with a razor-sharp part on the left side of his hair greeted us at the door. His name was Joe, and it turned out that he had organized the entire event. Joe's voice shook as he talked to Del. His face was suddenly void of any color as he expressed his admiration for the legendary figure who had just arrived from Chicago.

Joe offered to usher us into the theater to meet the students, but Del declined. "Take me to the can first," Del told him. "I need to take a piss."

After Del had relieved himself, we were taken into the theater where twenty-nine anxious students were awaiting our arrival. Joe delivered an introduction that elevated Del to mythic proportions. To his credit, Del graciously acknowledged the introduction and advised the students to forget everything Joe had just said. He wanted them to ignore who was teaching them and remember whom they were playing with.

"Let's see what you've got," he said to the students. "Get up on stage."

After three scenes had elapsed, Del interrupted them and instructed the improvisers to quit arguing. "I know that somebody's probably taught you to find the point of conflict, but I'm requesting that you never attempt to fucking find the fucking point of fucking conflict ever again," he said.

The performers looked a little shocked. The air conditioning was on in the theater, but the students seemed to break out in a sweat.

The action resumed on stage. Del interrupted just a few moments into the second scene. "Listen here," he started, "everybody is way over the top with all of these wacky characters. I don't want to see any more wild characters on this stage today. Be yourself and let your character be an extension of your personality. You should always wear your character like a thin veil.

"So throw away all your stock characters that you normally play and let's see you act like a human being. I have no desire to see some caricature that you think would be great on 'Saturday Night Live.' Don't waste my time."

The students stood on stage like they were about to jump out of their skin. Every time Del moved or shifted, the performers would snap their heads around and cringe, waiting for the other shoe to drop.

Joe stepped into the middle of the stage and began doing a scene with a curly-haired brunette wearing a pair of very short shorts and a plaid shirt. After a few quick lines, Joe informed the girl that she was a hooker and he wanted her to admit it.

Del erupted and jumped out of his seat. "Just stop. Just stop it already," he yelled. "If you don't stop wasting my time, I'm going to walk out of here and drive back to Chicago. I have yet to see one grounded relationship scene. They've all been about bizarre characters and frat-boy jokes, and I'm sick of it.

"You there, on the stage. What were you doing? Why did you make that girl turn into a hooker?"

Joe answered, "I thought she was playing the part of a hooker."

"I don't believe that's true. I think that it's very rare that a female improviser takes the stage with the intention of being a prostitute. Usually they're forced into those roles by inexperienced young men who have little imagination," Del said.

"Actually," he continued, "I think it was very clear to all of us that she was working in a garden until you barged in and called her a whore. Isn't that right?"

The girl nodded sheepishly.

"She obviously was working in a garden, which you completely ignored. So tell me, young man, why did you force her to play the part of a hooker?"

"I don't know," Joe answered. "I thought it would be funny."

"Well that blew up in your fucking face, didn't it?" Del asked him.

He turned to the entire class: "That is the last time that I ever want to hear that phrase again. Don't ever tell me that you did something because you thought it would be funny. Long-form improvisation isn't about the jokes and the cheap laughs. It's about people exploring and discovering situations and relationships. Humor will occur when our discovery is completely honest and ambiguous. Forget about the jokes and the bits and allow yourself to work with your scene partner so that the two of you can construct a relationship that is grounded and honest and real."

Joe looked like he was about to throw up. His eyes watered as he stepped back with the other students. I was rooting for a tear to drop down his cheek, but Joe managed to compose himself before it could happen.

The next half-hour was excruciating. Del stopped every scene and gave instructions. The students improvised like they were walking through a minefield. As they conversed with their scene partners, they would nervously glance to the seats, waiting for the axe to fall.

"My friends," Del shouted, "you are all under the misconception that you are the most important person on the stage. You are not. Your scene partner is. You need to consciously invest more concern and respect for each other on stage. Humility and deference will take you farther than arrogance and selfishness.

"You all need to settle down and build these scenes together. Too many of you are making too many decisions before you set a foot onstage. How are the two of you supposed to construct a scene when one of you has already determined the plot and direction of the scene? Stop thinking plot and start thinking more about relationship," Del continued.

I sat beside Del taking notes. He had encouraged me to keep detailed notes during classes so there would be some sort of documentation of his quotes and the lessons he had taught in recent years. I used the same notebook to write small journal entries detailing our weekly journeys. Del would pick up the notebook every so often and read the accounts of our trips that I'd chronicled.

"You really come off looking like an asshole," he'd laugh.

I was busy writing when Del snapped his fingers at me. "Get up there," he growled. I didn't understand what he wanted me to do. I looked at him confused.

"They don't get it. Get up on stage and show them how it's done," he ordered.

I set the notebook down and bashfully walked up the aisle of the theater toward the stage. Del ordered everyone off the stage and into the theater seats. I stood on the stage all by my lonesome.

"Where's the chick with the plaid shirt that played the gardener?" Del asked.

She meekly raised her hand and stood up so that Del could see her. Her skin was quite tanned, but her face flushed red at the sudden attention.

"You have good instincts," he told her. "Please take the stage with Jeff."

She walked onto the stage and stood beside me. I put out my hand and introduced myself. She leaned toward me and whispered that her name was Stephanie. I should have responded by telling her that it was nice to meet her. Instead I said, "Holy crap. You smell great." She had a subtle, sweet smell that floated from her.

"This is my apprentice, Jeff. He will now demonstrate what I've been trying to teach you for the last two hours," Del informed the students. And then as an aside to me, he added, "Don't fuck this up."

Stephanie took a deep breath and exhaled nervously. She took off her plaid shirt and tied it around her waist. She was wearing a short, tight tank top that covered very little of her flat, tan stomach. The tank top was low cut and white and had a tiny Cubs insignia right in the center of her chest. Del smiled and shrugged his shoulders. From that moment on, Del and I referred to her as Tank Top Girl.

We were given the suggestion of food poisoning, and we became two line cooks closing down a kitchen at the end of a night. Our characters found two plates of food covered in foil in the back of the refrigerator. After a great deal of rationalization, we decided to take a break from our work and eat the discovery. While eating, Tank Top Girl revealed that she had developed feelings for me since we had begun working with each other. I told her the feelings were mutual, and Tank Top Girl leaned in to kiss me. Suddenly she jumped up and ran offstage where her character began vomiting. She returned and announced that the mixture of food and emotions had caused her to throw up. We contemplated our situation and discussed the fact that work relationships are often difficult to maintain. We decided to take it slowly and allow the relationship to grow of its own volition. Suddenly Tank Top Girl grabbed my shirt and pulled me in to kiss her. Just as suddenly, she ran out of the room and vomited again. She returned and promised that there was nothing left inside of her to throw up. She asked if she could try to kiss me again. I said I very badly wanted to kiss her, but I was a little reticent after she had vomited twice. She gargled with Ranch dressing and turned to kiss me again. This time our lips connected and we kissed without incident. We pulled away from each other, smiling. I turned and walked out of the room and began vomiting.

Del called an end to the scene. Tank Top Girl and I sat on stage while Del and the students discussed the intricacies of our performance. The scene had lasted twenty-five minutes, and Del was effusive with his praise.

After the scene had been appropriately dissected, Del adjourned for an hour break. We were to resume at four o'clock. Del and I hadn't had a chance to eat lunch, so we ran across the street to grab a couple of sandwiches.

"That's why Chicago and ImprovOlympic are great," Del gushed. "There is a constant example of what we are teaching readily available. Every night there are shows and veteran improvisers who can show you exactly how it should be done. I'll take six improvisers from Chicago against the best six improvisers from around the world, and the quality, integrity, and professionalism from Chicago will win ten out of ten times."

We ate our sandwiches and discussed the Chicago style of improvisation. "This movement will continue to grow until we have influenced and contributed to performers around the world. They're not paying me that much money, but it's important that I do things like this so that we can spread the word and show everyone how long-form improvisation should be done," Del declared. He was excited.

We talked about my scene with Tank Top Girl. While it was a good scene and provided the students with an example of how Chicago style long-form was done, I had made several technical mistakes. Each time it seemed like the scene was progressing, I had introduced a problem that would keep the momentum from advancing. Instead of kissing her immediately, for example, I had stalled for a few moments.

"I was a little scared of her, Del," I confessed.

"With good reason," he chuckled. "She's beautiful, and she's wonderfully aggressive." I nodded in agreement.

"I bet you got an Ace of Diamonds when she took off that plaid shirt and revealed that Cubs emblem nestled in between those beautiful breasts," Del said.

I looked around to make sure that nobody had heard his last comments. "Don't be gross, Del," I admonished.

After the break, Tank Top Girl and I were instructed to do every other scene. The students would do a scene, then Tank Top Girl and I would edit and do a scene. Eventually Del felt comfortable enough to let her and me do every fifth scene.

After three hours of instruction, Del announced that the group was ready to do a show. A bar had been rented for the performance. There was to be an hour break so that the performers could rest and change clothes. Initially it had been determined that three groups of ten would perform together, but Del announced that he had decided to deviate from this plan. Instead the first group would contain fifteen people while the second group would have fourteen. The third team to perform that night would consist of Tank Top Girl and myself.

The students filed out of the theater baffled. After everyone had left, I protested to Del that I didn't think it was fair to the students for me to take away their stage time.

He shrugged his shoulders and said, "I don't care. Let them complain after they see the show. You'll have the best show of the evening, and it'll be the best example of what they need to strive for their shows to become."

I argued a bit more, and Del told me to shut up.

He reached into his dirty pocket and pulled out a large roll of cash. Joe had paid Del just before he left the theater, and Del had rolled the bills up in a rubber band and stuffed them into his pocket. He handed me thirty dollars and said, "Go find the Tank Top Girl and get yourselves something to eat. When you get done eating, go back to her dorm room and let her jump your bones."

"Del!" I yelled. "Don't be crass."

"Just do it and get it over with. The sexual tension between the two of you has everyone in the goddamn theater horny as a bunch of mutts in heat," he growled.

"I don't do that, Del," I snapped back at him.

"Why not?"

"I just don't. I have a little more respect for girls than that," I told him.

"Oh Lord. Respect is shit. Whatever happened to the good old days of free love? I would have sneaked away and fucked her in a closet already," Del bragged.

"And that's why nobody likes you!" I shouted.

"I'm just trying to help. It's obvious that the two of you dig each other. You should at least get a blow job out of it."

"Del. Quit!"

"If you don't do it, I will," he warned.

"With what?" I responded. "The hardest thing on you is that roll of cash in your pocket."

Del laughed and walked out of the theater. "I'm eating with the short fat kid that organized this thing. He didn't offer to pay for you, so you're on your own. I don't think he likes you," he told me.

"That's your fault," I told him.

"Nevertheless," Del giggled, "you better go find your girl-friend because you can't come with me."

He walked out of the theater and left me standing alone. I walked up the aisle and out the door where Tank Top Girl was waiting for me.

"The other guys took Del out to eat, and he said you were going to eat alone so I thought I'd see if you wanted to grab some pizza or something," she said as a waft of her perfume heightened every sense of my body.

We jumped into her Jeep Wrangler and drove to a pizza place that was close to where we were going to perform. I used the thirty dollars Del gave me to buy a pepperoni pizza, a Diet Coke for myself, and a light beer for Tank Top Girl.

We walked to the bar and arrived just as Del was giving in-structions to the two groups. Because we weren't performing until third, Tank Top Girl and I sat in the audience with Del to watch the first two shows. Del took the stage and spoke before each group was introduced. He intended to be brief, but he launched into anecdotes that rambled on and on.

The bar was packed and the first group amused the audi-ence greatly. Joe was in the second group. He struggled with the new concepts he had been taught earlier in the day, but the group put on a stellar show. Tank Top Girl and I stood next to the stage as Del stood in front of the packed theater telling everyone a story about freebasing with Richard Pryor. Tank Top Girl took my hand in hers and squeezed it.

After Del introduced us, we proceeded to do four scenes in forty-five minutes. The first scene started slowly as it took a few minutes for us to shake off our nerves. Once we put ourselves on solid footing, we picked up momentum and each scene progressively improved. The fourth scene ended with Tank Top Girl and I playing the roles of a baseball pitcher and a catcher who had slapped each other's butts after an important strikeout—except that their hands had lingered just a little too long on each other's rear ends.

The audience cheered as the lights went dark ending the show. All three groups came to the stage for a final curtain call, which was followed by another brief speech by Del. The performers mingled with the audience. I suddenly lost Tank Top Girl. Del appeared beside me and motioned for me to join him outside.

He looked at me scratching his beard. "I think we should get a hotel room for the night."

I was surprised that Del wanted to stay. He had a class on Sunday at noon, so we would have to get up very early to get back to Chicago. "I don't think that's a good idea, Del. We should probably get going pretty soon."

He slumped his shoulders, rolling his eyes. "Listen, you idiot. I'm trying to give you the opportunity to get laid. Go find that girl and go home with her, and I'll see you tomorrow."

I don't know why he was pushing me to sleep with the girl, but it was kind of touching how much he wanted me to find a girlfriend. "Thank you for trying to help, Del, but I just can't do that," I reminded him.

"Fine. Don't screw her, but at least go ahead and go through your namby-pamby relationship garbage. Don't walk away from it," he scolded me.

I appreciated the thought, but I knew it wouldn't work out. "We can't have a relationship, Del. We live in two different cities. I'm five years older than she is. I don't know if we even like each other."

"You are doing the same thing now that you were doing in your scenes this afternoon. Each time it seems like your life is progressing, you introduce a problem that will keep the momentum from advancing. Who cares if she vomited twice in that scene? She's insatiably sexy and you desperately wanted to kiss her. It's the same way right now. Who cares if she lives in a different city or if she's five years younger than you? She's amazingly sexy and you want to be with her, so go do it, you twit," he scolded me. "Improv is life. Life is improv."

He was right, and I knew it. I told him to wait for me in the truck so I could say goodbye to her. I walked into the theater. She was waiting for me at the door.

"I was scared that you left," she said and smiled.

I told her I had to take Del back to Chicago, but I'd really like to see her again. I asked her if she was ever going to visit Chicago. She said she would definitely come if I hung out with her and showed her around. We exchanged information and she stepped in close and hugged me goodbye. I turned and started to walk out to the truck. Del's words rang through my head, causing me to stop in my tracks. I turned around, and she smiled a seductive little grin. I stepped toward her and tugged at her little tank top, pulling her close to me. I reached my hand up and touched her face. I leaned in and kissed her, tasting her lip gloss and the beer on her breath.

"I like you a lot," I told her. "And, I'd really like you to come and visit." The words tumbling out of my mouth felt good. I wasn't putting up any roadblocks. I was just moving forward.

She grabbed my hair and tugged on it. "Thank God. I thought you were going to leave without saying anything." She kissed me again and made me promise to call her the next day.

When I arrived back at the truck, Del growled, "You better have at least kissed her."

"You'll never know," I told him.

He chuckled and positioned himself so that he could fall asleep as soon as we were on the road. Before we pulled out of the parking lot, I reached over and patted his arm. "Thank you, Del."

"You're welcome, retard," he answered.

I pulled away from campus and headed back to Chicago.

40

Cleaning Up

With the success of "SCTV" and Del's drug use growing increasingly dangerous, Second City and Del both recognized that his days with the comedy institution were again
numbered. Knowing of his avuncular relationships with many
"Saturday Night Live" cast members, NBC producer Jean Dou-
manian hired Del to run improv and acting sessions with the
cast from 1981 to 1983.

Most of the SNL cast had left the show after the 1980 season,
and NBC had hired a new cast of comedians. The result was a
lackluster show that struggled in the ratings. On New Year's Day
1981, Del was brought in to try to revitalize the program. During
the week he worked with Second City; each Thursday he flew to
New York "on loan" to "Saturday Night Live" to assist with the
show and help whip the actors into shape.

But the cast members didn't respond to Del's direction.
They weren't very good at taking criticism, and struggled with
his teaching. He worked tirelessly with the actors, writers, and
producers, but his efforts had little effect on the abysmal quality of the show's writing, and the cast never gelled.

Second City alums Tim Kazurinsky, Mary Gross, Brian
Doyle-Murray, and Robin Duke were all cast members during

Del's tenure at "Saturday Night Live." Del was officially employed as "house metaphysician." The fierce devotion of his high-profile students (John Belushi, Bill Murray, Gilda Radner, and Dan Aykroyd) and the current cast encouraged the network to keep Del in its employ. But his dependency on drugs ultimately convinced NBC not to extend his contract.

The show's producers had brought Del aboard to help cement a cast that had become worried—either that the show was about to be canceled or that they were about to be fired. As it turned out, they were fired. NBC brought in an entirely new cast the next season, salvaging only two young stars, Eddie Murphy and Joe Piscopo.

Del wasn't surprised that "Saturday Night Live" let him go. The drug situation at the show was out of control, and Del was a notorious abuser. While his talents were useful to the program, his constant influx of drugs was not. It was in both party's interests that the relationship end.

All this became too apparent when Del's highest-profile student overdosed. On March 5, 1982, John Belushi died from a lethal injection of cocaine and heroin, a mixture called a speedball. Or at least that was what Del had called it when he first introduced it to Belushi during the filming of *The Blues Brothers* in Chicago.

"I like the man's style," Belushi had said of Del. "He can create with you, unlike so many directors. He can motivate you."

Belushi's death devastated Del. Everyone had seen that Belushi was out of control, and Del had remarked to other friends that John was the "worst type of junkie. He couldn't choose what he wanted to be addicted to. Was it food, was it coke, was it heroin? He couldn't decide. He was sloppy and irresponsible, and it killed him."

Other of Del's friends had died from drug overdose. But after Belushi's death Del realized that he was moving down the
same path that his prized former student had traveled. He had
often contemplated suicide and had come close to overdosing
himself, but he now came to realize that his work was not finished, that there was still more he wanted to accomplish.

"We went to John's memorial service at St. John the Divine
at One-hundred-twelfth Street, and I was already high," Del
recalled. "I had shot up just before we left. I watched John's
brother Jim speak, and I started to feel myself break down.
Paul Shafer and a couple of other people played 'For a
Dancer,' and in my heart I reconciled that I needed to make a
change. There was a hypodermic needle in my shaving kit, so
after we left the service I took it out and threw it out in the
street.

"I decided to give up drugs as a tribute to John Belushi. I
figured something good had to come out of his death."

Del battled guilt and depression for the next year and began to combat his addictions. He had read Yvonne Frost's book
A Witch's Guide to Psychic Healing and corresponded with her.
The book described the power of spiritual healing in the Wiccan religion. Besides being a member of Mensa, Frost was a
founder of the Church and School of the Wicca. With the help
of priests and witches in the pagan community, Del tried to
kick his drug habit.

While in Toronto directing a show for Second City, he took
part in a "banishing ceremony." With a rock in one hand and a
candle in the other, he and the other witches tossed heroin, cocaine, valium, and other examples of his addictions into a large
fire. Then they leaped through the flames and danced to ex-
haustion. Three weeks later he was clean. He readily admitted
that magical spirits hadn't eliminated his addiction, but he said

he had accepted the images of the universe of the pagans, to the point where he was allowing them to work in him. Del relished in his new religion, which soon became a way of life. He learned about survival and the ethical use of natural innate powers.

While Del was working diligently to end his drug usage, his relationship with Second City soured once again. The problem was his frequent disagreement with Bernie Sahlins over improv being an art form.

Sahlins stood firm in the idea that improv was a means to an end, a way to develop sketch material. In *Something Wonderful Right Away*, he tells Jeffrey Sweet, "I think that Viola's book is wrong and that Paul's emphases are wrong in the sense that I do not believe that we are leading to another form or part of the classical theater." He goes on to call improvisation "a functional device to achieve a goal other than itself. Just as fencing is. I know there are people who will want to string me up for saying it, but improvisation is a tool for arriving at . . . Second City material. It hasn't proven viable for anything else." In his own book, *Days and Nights at the Second City*, Sahlins notes, "[Del] maintained that it was indeed an art form, deserving to be elevated to presentational status. I felt that to do so was a self-indulgence, that improvisation elevated to a form of presentation failed most of the time, that any scene could benefit from editing, concision, and shaping."

Their philosophical differences destroyed their working relationship. Officially Del's departure was described as a mutual decision. In Del's mind, he knew the real reasons he was no longer working at 1616 North Wells: drugs and improv. His obsession with both had put him out of a job once more.

Del began teaching workshops again, including weekly classes at a bar named Cross-Currents. After one of his classes

Charna Halpern approached Del and asked him to begin teaching workshops for her theater company, ImprovOlympic. She had co-founded the company with David Shepherd, one of the co-founders of the Compass Players, but she was not happy with their association and had decided to end it. With a little persuasion and a bag of weed, Charna was able to convince Del to work with her group. The partnership would last for the rest of his life.

After a long struggle, Del's use of drugs had dwindled to marijuana and cigarettes, both of which he believed to be harmless. He was teaching regularly for Charna and ImprovOlympic and prompting a great deal of attention around town. He became a semi-regular performer for the Goodman Theatre, appearing in *A Christmas Carol*, in Elaine May's one-act play *Hotline*, and in *The Time of Your Life*. For his role as Kit Carson in *The Time of Your Life*, Del received a nomination for the Joseph Jefferson award, Chicago's version of the Tony.

In 1985 he won accolades for his portrayal of Polonius in Robert Fall's radical version of *Hamlet*, set in Richard Nixon's White House and staged at the Wisdom Bridge Theatre. He received the Jefferson Award that year for best actor.

Del's performance caught the eye of several agents; he chose Elizabeth Geddes to represent him. She began sending him to auditions for movies that were casting in Chicago, and he landed roles in several films.

Charna, acting as Del's manager, helped him get his life in order. Over the years he had neglected to pay taxes, so he owed a substantial amount of money to the United States government. Bill Murray stepped forward and loaned Del the money to pay the IRS. Murray had already done several highly successful films, including *Meatballs*, *Caddyshack*, and *Stripes*. A year earlier he had also bailed out his friends and fellow Second City alums Dan

Aykroyd and Harold Ramis when he took over a role in a movie that was intended for John Belushi. Murray played the role of Peter Venkman in *Ghostbusters*, originally written for John.

Several years later Del sent Bill Murray a check to repay the loan. One day the phone rang, as I visited Del and he asked me to answer it. I recognized Murray's voice immediately and stalled for a few minutes while Del went to the bathroom with the door open. Del eventually took the phone from me and spoke for a few minutes with his former student. Del praised him for his role in *Rushmore*, which had just been released. When Del hung up, he told me that if I were ever to become famous, he wanted me to be like Bill Murray.

I asked Del what Murray had said. "He sent back my check. He made some sort of excuse about paying me for some project that we'd worked on together several years ago, but it's a ruse to hide his generosity. That guy is, and always will be, a friend and a gentleman."

After his success in *Hamlet*, the next few years were the most productive of Del's career. His partnership with Charna was attracting students from around the country to the ImprovOlympic. He continued to star in *A Christmas Carol* at the Goodman during the holiday season. While his theater career thrived, he also started to work in films.

In 1986 he played a zoologist in *First Step*, a forgettable film that starred Judd Hirsch and the Chicago actor John Mahoney. To Del it was refreshing to be in front of a camera again. Appearing in movies and on TV shows gave him a validation he had longed for.

The following year he played a small role as an English professor in the wildly popular *Ferris Bueller's Day Off*. Del's lecturing to his bored students in the movie brought him consistent recognition by fans of the film.

A whole new audience now learned about Del. Beside his forays into movies, theater, and improvisation, he began writing comic books with fellow actor and playwright John Ostrander. The two of them had teamed up to write for *Munden's Bar* at First Comics. DC Comics approached Del and John to write a horror comic for mature audiences. *Wasteland* was the result, and it became a huge success for DC. It featured some of Del's most bizarre and twisted autobiographical stories. DC Comics put out sixteen issues of *Wasteland*. Del developed a cult following among the graphic-novel crowd.

In 1987 Del starred in *The Big Town* with Matt Dillon and *The Untouchables* with Sean Connery and Kevin Costner. Del's role as Deacon Daniels in *The Big Town* was the biggest part he had played in a major motion picture thus far. He traveled to the set every morning with Dillon and struck up a nice relationship with him. In his kitchen, over his sink, Del hung a portrait of himself that Dillon had painted during the filming of the movie. He was very fond of it.

"I will pay you the courtesy of being frank," was the line that instigated Del's scene-stealing turn in *The Untouchables*. He played the part of a sleazy alderman who tried to bribe Eliot Ness.

Del had roles in several more films, most notably *The Blob*, *Fat Man and Little Boy*, and the Dana Carvey flop *Opportunity Knocks*. The achievement that meant the most to him, though, was being asked to direct Second City's fifty-first revue, "The Gods Must Be Lazy." The show received mixed reviews, and the audience was confused as Del applied some of his Harold theories toward the organization of the revue. It departed from the typical Second City format, and it took a while for the audience to catch on. Later revues, "Pinata Full of Bee's" and "Citizen Gates," borrowed liberally from Del's long-form theories with better results.

The first thing Del did when he went in to direct "The Gods Must Be Lazy" was to fire the entire cast. He brought in several of his ImprovOlympic students who were also employed by Second City in their touring companies. Chris Farley and Tim Meadows were two of the students he selected to perform in his triumphant return to 1616 North Wells Street. Continuing Del's impressive streak of discovering and training exceptional comedic talent, Farley and Meadows would both move on to "Saturday Night Live." Farley would hit it big in movies as well, starring in several successes like *Wayne's World*, *Tommy Boy*, and *Black Sheep*.

Farley stopped by ImprovOlympic often to sit in on the Monday night "Armando Diaz" show, the showcase performance for the theater's veterans and alumni. Del often taught on Monday nights and would ask me to sit in on the class to watch his teaching style and get some stage time improvising under his tutelage. On my first Monday night class I witnessed a sad exchange between the former pupil and his disappointed instructor.

Farley bounded down the ramp and interrupted the class to say hi to Del. Del informed him that there was a class in progress and he could speak to him later. Farley awkwardly apologized and asked Del if he would come up and watch the second half of the show when the class was finished.

"I understand that three weeks ago when you performed upstairs you weren't getting any laughs, so you pulled down your pants and showed everyone your fat ass," Del told him.

"Aw, Del, my ass isn't that big anymore. I lost weight," Farley responded.

"That's not the point," Del scolded him. "I have no desire to watch you ignore everything I taught you. If you can perform your characters with honesty and integrity, I would come and watch you, but unfortunately I don't think that's going to happen. Not everything you say has to be funny. You'll be a much better performer when you realize that."

The class sat there in shock. No one expected this huge celebrity to be scolded in front of us. The entire time Del spoke, Farley smiled, nodded, and fidgeted. Once Del was finished, Farley responded, "Oh Del, you're so funny. You always yell at me. Come up, okay?" And with that he disappeared.

Del sighed, "He didn't hear a word I said to him."

He was right. I drove Del home and returned to the theater to talk to the people who had seen the show. It turned out that Farley had been in a dreadful scene that was getting no response from the audience, so he had taken off his shirt and started humping the leg of his scene partner.

While Farley seemed oblivious to Del's direction, throngs of students worshiped him as faithful acolytes. Bob Odenkirk, who went on to be part of the successful HBO program "Mr. Show," was deeply affected by the legendary teacher. "His vision of the creative life was exciting," Odenkirk said. "But more important, it was real human. It wasn't so much what he said—it was, here was a guy who'd actually done it, and he was happy about his life."

After Del directed the Second City show, he and Charna began looking for a permanent space for ImprovOlympic. To be recognized as a legitimate entity, they needed the stability of an immutable home.

41

Sex Wars

The new Harold schedule at ImprovOlympic was out, and my team, Deep Schwa, was listed as a house team. We were now scheduled consistently on Friday and Saturday evenings. Spoo was motoring along nicely, and improv as a whole was going smoothly for me.

Del's current class was a few weeks away from putting up its new form. Del was clearly excited about it. The class was composed equally of men and women, and he decided that it would be the perfect opportunity to have an improvisational battle of the sexes. He called the show "Sex Wars"; it would focus on the differences between men and women. He asked me to come to the last three classes and do the show Saturdays at midnight.

I agreed, though I was a little worried about committing to it. After I had been to one of the classes, I was even less enthusiastic about taking part in the production.

"It's not a battle between men and women," I told him as we shopped in the produce section of the Jewel at Southport and Addison. "It's really a battle of sex stories between men and women."

Del picked up a carton of blueberries and his eyes danced. "Isn't it great?"

I shrugged. "I don't know, Del. I don't know if I want to be involved with a show where people are trying to outdo each other's stories of sexual exploits."

He insisted that I continue with the show. "That's why I asked you to do it. I know that when the show turns raunchy, you'll rein it in and bring it back to grounded, intelligent scene work."

Del had asked the Tall Blonde Girl to take part in the show too. She had been asked for the opposite reason he had asked me: she was voluble and explicit in talking about her sexual experiences and conquests.

"She's deliciously and delightfully dirty," Del described her as we made our way to the long checkout lines. "I think you just want to hear her and the other women talk about their sex lives," I accused him.

He chuckled but didn't deny it. "It's more than that. I asked her to be a part of the show because she's a surprisingly good improviser."

I was loading the groceries onto the counter and stopped suddenly. "Why do you say, 'She's a surprisingly good improviser'?"

He reached into his wallet to pay for his haul of fruit, vegetables, and bread. "I always find it surprising when I see a woman improvise well," he said matter-of-factly.

"Why?" I asked, baffled.

"Because, my dear boy, women aren't funny." He flashed a smile.

He took his receipt from the cashier and walked toward the doors to the parking lot. He was physically unable to carry any of the groceries because his emphysema would cause him to launch into an attack. He normally waited for me to gather up all his purchases. I grabbed the bags and hurried to catch up with him.

Del had made this statement earlier a couple of times in class, but no one had challenged it. I was ready to do battle with him now, but I couldn't catch up. By the time I did, he was standing beside the truck. The window was still broken, and Del was trying to brush off the glass that just didn't seem to go away.

"You don't really think that women aren't funny, Del," I said as I set the grocery bags into the flatbed of the truck.

"Yes," he nodded, "I do. I think men are naturally funnier than women. I think women try too hard to make themselves funny and don't use their intelligence. Instead they put on a funny face or a crazy voice and demean themselves to get a laugh."

"Oh Del," I sighed. "I really disagree with you."

"That's your prerogative, but you'd be wrong," he said smirking.

"It's such an archaic point of view, Del. I think you say things like that just to be controversial."

He smirked again and answered, "That's also your prerogative, but you'd be wrong once again."

We drove in silence for a while. Del sensed I was angry, so he defended his position.

"Look, I'm not saying that across the board women aren't funny. I'm just saying that in general women aren't funny. Elaine May is brilliant and has always had more talent than every man she's worked with. Tina Fey is outstanding, and so are Rachel Dratch and the chick that's with UCB. When women are intelligent and wear their characters like a thin veil, they can stand toe to toe with any man. Sadly, they try too hard. The audience walks away shaking their heads because most women come across as dumb and annoying."

I stared ahead and drove. He was trying to debate his point, but I wasn't going to argue with him. I told him that he was now trying to justify his statements.

"You know who backs up my point?" he asked. "Women."

He continued, "They'll argue with me until they're blue in

the face, but if you talk to a female audience member after a show, she'll spend her time criticizing the female performers. Most women find woman performers to be unfunny. They would prefer to watch men play than other women.

"As a whole, audiences come in with a distaste for female comedians. Because of that handicap, women spend all their time onstage trying to get approval. Approval from the audience, approval from their teachers and directors, and approval from their fellow performers. The women who succeed are the women who refuse to be affected by everyone else around them. They play with confidence and intelligence and subtlety."

I tried to keep from commenting, but I couldn't help it. "Del," I challenged, "don't you think that things have changed in this community so that's no longer the case? People see Rachel and Amy and they've learned from them. And I think it goes both ways. I think people see how incredible Tina Fey and Stephnie Weir are, and they get an appreciation for women and how funny they can be. I just think we've progressed to the point that blanket statements like 'Women aren't funny' can't be justified any more."

I hadn't won my argument, but at least he considered my points.

"To some degree, you're right," he said. "I used to say that I didn't think black people were funny, but as time has progressed I've modified my feelings about that."

I was appalled, but that was a whole can of worms I didn't want to get into.

"There seems to be a sudden surge of quality, female improvisers that have appeared in our community," Del continued. "Hell, that Molly girl is the best improviser in the Lindbergh Babies, and that team is made up of superstars.

"At some point I imagine I'll probably have to modify my 'Women aren't funny' statement. Hopefully I'll die before that happens," he said and smiled. He had a gap between his teeth, which made him look sadistically demented.

I was a little surprised by the time we arrived at his house. He had conceded somewhat, and I hadn't expected that. He hadn't changed his mind, but he had acknowledged that times were changing and that he would soon have to alter his opinion. He had also explained that much of his opinion had to do with society's image of female performers, which I hadn't heard him say before.

I started to think that Del was growing in character in his old age.

He must have read my mind. As he got out of the truck, he leaned in through the broken window and said, "If I do change my mind on women, thank God we'll always have the Mexicans and the fags to fuck everything up."

42

Santa Claus

A new Ikea store had opened, and Del wanted to see it. We rumbled down the highway to the suburbs, our eyes on the skies. The window of the truck still wasn't fixed, and it was threatening rain.

Arriving in the parking lot in Schaumburg, we drove around for fifteen minutes looking for a place to park. Del griped and complained as people cut us off and sped up and down the aisles looking for precious parking spots. We finally found one and slid into the yellow-lined space. When we walked into the store, Del was instantly angry. The place was bustling with people.

We walked through the store while Del denounced everything as pretentious and unusable. "Yuppie, crappy, bullshit," he decried every chance he could. "All this furniture looks like it was built for freaking midgets."

I needed a new bed frame and walked around looking for a nice-sized bed that would fit into my budget. Del watched me test out the models. I could tell he was putting some serious consideration into buying one for himself. At first he nagged me to hurry, but when I finally made a decision to buy one, he talked me into going back for a different frame.

I tried to talk him into buying a bed frame for himself, but he wanted to wait to see if I liked mine.

Once I ordered the frame, we had to go to a waiting area to have it brought to us. I went to the parking lot and brought the truck around to the loading area. The parking lot was in such a constant state of congestion that it took quite a while for me to get back to the loading area.

Del was standing guard over my new bed frame. I could see him from the cab of my truck, but it seemed like I would never reach the spot. As I sat in traffic watching him, I witnessed an interesting event. Several children began gathering around him while he stood there oblivious to their existence. One of the kids reached up and tugged at his shirt, and Del bent down and listened. Then he stood up straight and responded loudly enough for all the kids to hear. I arrived just as all the children ran away screaming. A woman beside Del angrily said something to him, but Del continued to stare straight ahead. I read his lips as he responded with a "Fuck off."

I jumped out of the truck and began to load my frame onto the truck. "What happened?" I asked Del as he opened the door and sat down.

The lady in the loading area answered, "Those children asked if he was Santa Claus, and he told them he was Santa Claus's brother and he had killed Santa Claus in his sleep. Then he told them to go tell all their friends that Santa Claus is dead."

I stifled a laugh and continued loading while the woman yelled that he was an evil monster.

"Is that your grandfather?" she yelled.

"No," I assured her. "Santa Claus was actually my grandfather, but that man in my truck killed him. So now he's my foster grandpa." I could hear Del laughing in the truck.

"Both of you are sick, twisted deviants," she screamed. She continued yelling at me, but I walked away.

The clouds darkened as I settled in behind the wheel. "Why did you do that?" I asked Del as I started the truck and pulled out of the loading area.

Without a bit of remorse, Del replied, "I hate children."

After ten minutes of being stuck in the parking lot, we finally reached the highway and left Schaumburg behind us. We both kept checking the rear-view mirrors to monitor a storm that was quickly forming in the west.

Just as it appeared we would escape the rain, the skies opened. Thunder, lightning, and rain crashed down on us. The open passenger's side window acted like an open drain as the rain flooded into the cab of the truck. Del scooted over to where he was almost on top of me, but we were both soon drenched.

Twenty-five minutes later the rain stopped as we pulled off the Kennedy and onto Belmont Avenue.

"Fucking karma!" Del exclaimed as the rain slowed to sparse drizzle.

My new wooden frame bed was soaking wet. Because it was unfinished wood, I was afraid I had wasted a whole lot of money.

"So pneumonia is your newest mode of assassination," Del said as he tried to wipe the rain off his glasses.

"If it is, I've screwed myself," I answered.

I thought of the bright side as we drove the rest of the way to Del's place: at least the rain had given him a bath.

43

The Del Game

People around the ImprovOlympic played a game called the "Del Game." To play the game a person would name a random celebrity and a random drug. Everyone else would then do their best Del impression to create an outlandish and bizarre situation where the celebrity, the drug, and Del had interacted.

People would come up with some ridiculous, grotesque situations, but no one could match the master. The real situations Del described outdid any that people invented.

My friend Jackie was performing in the Annoyance Theater's production of *The Manson Family Chronicles*. It was well cast, smart, and fun. I had really liked the show and told Del about it. I suggested that he would really enjoy it.

"I don't have to see it, I lived it," he said as he sat barefoot in his kitchen eating out of a bowl. It looked like dried grains of some sort. I figured he just didn't have any milk for his cereal. "I remember when Charlie and his freaks showed up at Brian Wilson's house. I was there with Jerry Garcia and Wavy Gravy, and I swear that little asshole stole my stash. Not impressed."

He went on to describe another party where Manson and his friends were tossed out because they were too rowdy. "I talked to him for a little while because we both shared a mutual friend, L. Ron Hubbard. Manson had just become a Scientologist. I was trying to talk to him about Dianetics, but all the little bastard wanted to talk about was whether I could introduce him to Keith Relf of the Yardbirds so that Manson could play one of his songs for him. I was so high on Quaaludes that I almost mistakenly fucked one of his female henchmen. Two days later they used Sharon Tate for wallpaper."

He then went on a rant about how he was annoyed that Hugh Romney, also known as Wavy Gravy, had gotten a great deal of fame and attention because of his ridiculously cute name. Ben and Jerry had named an ice cream flavor after him, and it drove Del crazy. I told him he was jealous. We sat for a few minutes trying to come up with ideas for an ice cream using Del's name. I suggested Junkie Jamboree, which would be a mixture of heroin, chunks of 'shrooms, urine, dirty socks, ice cream, and sprinkles of schizophrenic tendencies. When he laughed a little too hard, I realized that something was amiss.

"What are you eating?" I asked Del as heaping spoonfuls entered his mouth.

"Pot. You want some?"

He was already too high to roll a joint or put it into his bong, so he was eating it dry.

"That's disgusting," I told him. "That's got to be so dry. How are you swallowing it?"

He giggled and shrugged.

We hadn't gone to run our errands, but it was obvious that we weren't about to get anything done that day. I told him I was leaving, shut the door, and headed out. It must not have registered, because as I made my way down the stairs I could hear him telling a story about skinny-dipping with Yul Brynner in Bob Newhart's swimming pool.

The "Del Game" was his game. Everyone else was an amateur.

44

Wrigley Field

We'd had a rather uneventful afternoon of errands. As I dropped Del off in front of his house, he stood holding the door open for a few minutes.

"I was thinking about it last night," he started, "and I can't remember having ever gone to a Cubs game. Usually there are way too many people at those things. I'd rather sit home and get high and watch it. But I figure it's one of those things I should experience, and I'm really interested in this young pitcher that the Cubs have right now.

"Would you know how to go about getting us some tickets to see this Kerry Wood pitch?" he asked me. He added, "I'll pay for it."

He definitely had come to the right place. I was a certified Die-Hard Cubs Fan. From the time I was a young boy I had watched every game I could possibly see. My fondest memories are of the summers I spent watching the games with my dad on our couch. Jody Davis was my favorite player; my dad loved Ron Cey. I'd root for Jody to hit a home run every game; my dad always wanted Ron Cey to try and beat out a throw in the infield. Cey was short and stubby and looked like a penguin when he ran. My dad loved to see Ron Cey run.

"I can get tickets for us," I told Del. He asked me how much it would cost, then he reached into his wallet and threw the money on the seat of the truck.

"I can't walk too far, so try to get something that will be comfortable for me," he announced as he stood standing in his long-sleeve denim button-down shirt with a black T-shirt and blue jeans.

The following Thursday he was wearing the same outfit as we snaked our way through the crowd at Wrigley Field. It was a bright, pleasant summer afternoon, and we had arrived in plenty of time to take our seats. As we climbed the stairs and the field came into view, he stopped and stared and uttered, "Breathtaking."

It was so sunny that Del took off his denim shirt and sat there in his black T-shirt. "Get some sun on my track marks," he said loud enough for everyone to hear. I had bought tickets for us to sit in the family section because that required Del to walk the fewest steps and also gave us better access to leave when we were ready. The family section is located just beside the left-field foul pole and consists of three long rows of seats. I put us on the end next to the wall so that Del wouldn't have to worry about getting up and down to let people pass. We didn't have anyone sitting in front of us, so that was also a positive.

I didn't stop to think that the conversation between Del and me might not be "family section" appropriate.

Del was surprised just how much he enjoyed the entire experience. He cheered, booed, and ate as much ballpark food as I could buy. "I'd love to have a beer, but I know it would make me sick," he said ruefully as he sat around watching everyone in the other sections drinking. Alcohol was forbidden in the family section, but there was another reason Del couldn't have a beer.

Throughout his years, Del had put every drug imaginable into his body, but cigarettes and alcohol were ultimately the two that caused him the most problems. Emphysema from smoking had crippled him in the past few years, and he truly believed that years of alcohol abuse had accelerated his aging process and helped deteriorate his body. He had told me, "The sad thing is, I can't remember half the drugs I did because I was too drunk to know what I was putting in my body. It's annoying just how much good shit I wasted."

After his aversion therapy cure, anytime he had any sort of alcohol, he would be physically ill for days.

Even without the beer, Del was having a good time. It surprised many people that Del had expressed an interest in going to an athletic event. I knew better. While Del was passionate about movies and theater and things that were considered artistic, he loved sports and talked about them often in class. Most of the classes I took with him started with the statement, "I got really high and watched football all day yesterday, and that reminded me that improvisation is . . ."

The Cubs were seven games behind Houston, but they were playing well and were four games over the .500 mark. A day earlier Sammy Sosa had hit his thirty-fourth home run of the season. Kerry Wood was a hard-throwing rookie pitcher who was setting strikeout records. Cub fever was in full bloom, and Del had caught it.

By the eighth inning the Cubs had the game well in hand. When Kerry Wood was taken out, Del started talking about leaving the ballpark so that we could avoid traffic. We decided we would leave after the Cubs batted in the eighth.

We were leaving the field when Del and I witnessed an interesting event. An older gentleman walked up from the steps of one of the entrances and stopped to talk to a security guard.

We noticed him immediately because he was wearing a suit and smoking a cigar.

Del pointed at him and elbowed me. "Why does that bastard get to smoke in here?"

Several other security guards approached the man and talked to him. They nodded and spoke on walkie-talkies, then scattered back to their positions and left the man to his lonesome. He took a plastic bag out of his pocket and walked toward the wall next to the field. Cramming the cigar into his mouth, he used both hands to open the seal of the plastic bag. As he held up the bag, I could see the contents.

"What's he have in there?" Del asked as the man suddenly flipped the bag over and a grey powder fluttered onto the field. The man stood taking in the moment, then made the sign of the cross. He kissed a necklace he was wearing, quietly walked to the exit, and left the ballpark. It seemed that Del and I were the only two people who had seen what the man had done.

"Jesus," Del sighed. "That'll put a downer on your little trip to the ballgame. Your team wins, but you've got to spread your buddy's cremated remains over the field before you leave."

We sat for some time before Del finally spoke. "This is a pretty nice place for a final resting spot."

I nodded but didn't have much to say.

"I read an article in a magazine about a procedure in which the head is removed from the body, and then it's boiled so that the skin can be removed and the skull preserved," he told me.

The look on my face was a mixture of puzzlement and horror. "That's disgusting," I told him.

He smiled and nodded his head with glee. "I know. Isn't it great?" he cackled.

"Why would anyone do that?" I asked him. He seemed a little too happy with my appalled reaction.

"I don't know why other people do it. I'm doing it so that the Goodman Theatre can use it in their next production of *Hamlet*."

"What do you mean, 'You're doing it'?" I asked him.

"When Hamlet is in the graveyard, he picks up a skull and pronounces, 'Ah, Yorick, I knew him well.' I'm going to have them cut off my head, peel off my skin, and give my skull to the Goodman," he said with a gleam in his eye.

I could tell he was serious. "Why would you do that?"

"No one else has performed in a play after they've died, and I want to be the first person to do it," he said without any remorse.

"What are they going to do with the rest of your body?"

He lit up again, "I'm going to be cremated, and Melanie Blue's going to eat my ashes."

People around us were getting uncomfortable. Melanie was one of Del's former students; it would be an understatement to call her eccentric. She had told Del that she had eaten her husband's ashes when he died, and Del had fallen in love with the idea. He had asked her if she would eat his ashes after he passed on. She promised that she would.

On the field, Rod Beck was brought in to get the save as the Cubs cruised to a victory. Deciding to get a head start, Del and I made our way down the stairs and out to the street. We had parked the truck in the garage of a friend of mine who lived a couple of blocks away.

We talked about the game and Del thanked me for going with him. I tried to avoid the whole death topic, but he steered the conversation back to his demise. He wanted to make sure I knew that he was serious. His skull was going to the Goodman, and Melanie would eat his ashes.

"I'm going to do it, you know," he said. "It's going to happen."

I didn't argue. There was no doubt in my mind that he was right.

45

Charna

My several friends in Del's classes all told me that he talked about our trips each week. After the trip to Ikea, one of his students offered to fix the window of the truck for free. We would only have to pay for the glass.

At the garage where the student worked, Del and I sat in the air-conditioned waiting room while he replaced the window. It felt like Del and I spent most of our time together in waiting rooms.

The previous day Del and Charna had got into a bit of a spat. Del had tried to talk her into installing video cameras in the theater so they could tape all their shows, but she had refused. He was frustrated, but he conceded that it was her theater and she could do anything she wanted. From that, we stumbled onto the relationship between Del and Charna. It was a topic I was itching to talk about, but I could never bring myself to ask him about their association.

"I'm quite fond of her," he announced, and looked away so that I couldn't make eye contact.

"What do you mean by 'fond'?" I asked, trying to draw out more information.

"Not romantically, which is what you're trying to infer," he answered. "We passed that by a long time ago. I think I thought at one point there might be something there romantically, but I don't believe she ever harbored those types of feelings for me."

I was careful not to prod too much because I didn't want him to clam up.

"Her parents even thought there was something going on between us. They took us out to dinner to tell us that they approved of the relationship," Del said and smiled. "I told them, 'Thanks, but no thanks. I could never marry a Jew,' and then I got the hell out of there."

I looked through the glass to see how much longer the window was going to take. I was ready to kill any mechanic who walked through the door and interrupted this conversation.

"I watched her date other people, and I had my flings and wondered if the two of us would settle down with each other. Eventually all of those kinds of feelings went away. We've settled into a matronly relationship. If anything romantic had ever happened between us, there's no doubt we would have fucked all of this up." He sighed and continued. "I really like her current boyfriend. I think there's a good chance it's going to work out for them. I mean, he looks like a girl and needs to cut his hair, but Charna likes it so that's all that matters."

"I can't imagine the two of you together," I told him.

"It wouldn't have worked. I don't know that either of us ever seriously entertained any thoughts that it be a realistic consideration," he said. "I don't know what I was thinking back then. She's loud, irrational, and remarkably stubborn. Looking back at it, though, I don't know that I've ever cared for or loved anyone more than that woman." He chewed on his lip and looked at me.

"She saved my life, you know," he said. "If she hadn't taken care of me the past twenty years, I would have died in an alley somewhere."

I'd heard the story before, but he recited it again. Charna had just ended her partnership with David Shepherd, one of the co-founders of The Compass, when she ran into Del and convinced him to come and teach classes for her. Del, who was down to his last few dollars, jumped at the opportunity to teach regularly and get a semi-steady paycheck.

Charna based her theater on Del's teachings and abandoned the competitive short-form games in favor of Del's long-form performance pieces. As Del's reputation grew, students began flocking to the ImprovOlympic to study with him. He was broke and a hard-core drug abuser, but Charna looked past all that and saw the genius behind the man. While everyone else had given up on him and dismissed him as a lost cause, Charna gave him a job and convinced him to stop doing drugs. She saved his life. He would be loyal to her forever.

When I saw the mechanic walking toward the waiting room, I knew this conversation would end. This was a window that Del rarely opened. I knew it would close and neither of us would ever speak of this again.

"Twenty years. I can't believe I haven't killed her yet," he grumbled as we stood up to get the truck.

We jumped in the car and headed north on Ashland. As we stopped at a light, Del grabbed the handle to roll the window down. It was stuck, so Del applied a little pressure. The window shattered into a thousand pieces.

We were shocked. We considered going back to have it replaced and decided against it. Instead we went to the nearest hardware store, and once again I taped plastic to the window.

"I should have known better. Why would I ever have expected a bad improviser to be able to put together a window," Del sighed. We patched the window together in the parking lot and drove away.

That weekend Charna relented, installing the movie cameras that Del had wanted. Within days of their installation, the theater was burglarized and the cameras were stolen.

46

The Information Superhighway

"Do you have a computer?" Del asked me as we ambled down Clark Street to the grocery store.

"Yeah," I answered. "I've had one for several years."

"Do you get on the internet with it?" he asked. I squinted at him because I couldn't understand where this was leading.

"I've thought about getting a computer," he told me to my surprise. "The only thing I want to do is check out the internet and use e-mail, so I don't really know that I need a computer."

Del had read about a web-based system that catered to people who wanted to use the internet but didn't want to invest thousands of dollars in a computer. It plugged into the television and used a 56K modem. It was called Web-TV and seemed perfect for him.

I told Del that Best Buy had the system, which I didn't think was very expensive. Upon hearing that, he decided he wanted to forgo our trips to the grocery store and the pet store in order to buy the equipment that would catapult Del Close onto the Information Superhighway.

We bought the system and returned to Del's place so that I could connect it for him. I was used to setting up computers, so the installation of the Web-TV was pretty simple. Once all the wires and cables were connected, Del entered all his information into the system so that he had a monthly subscription.

I explained how to surf from site to site and showed him how to send e-mail. His first e-mail was to me:

"Dear Firecracker,
You're quite the douche bag.
Del"

It was now growing late, and a light rain had settled on the city. I could smell the first drops through the open window. Afternoon had turned to evening as Del and I played with his new toy.

The different features tickled Del. He traveled from website to website and was more and more amazed each time he landed somewhere new. We stumbled across a site that was set up solely for Web-TV users—an archived library of radio programs from the forties and fifties. "Life of Riley" caught Del's eye, and he urged me to click on it. He had thought that by clicking on it, a general description of the show would pop up. He was shocked to suddenly have the show playing from his television set.

As the theme song sounded through the living room, Del sank back into the couch. He closed his eyes and put his hand over his mouth. When the theme ended, the actors launched right into the program. Del gasped.

He opened his eyes and shook his head in disbelief. "Is it the whole show?"

"I think so," I answered. I looked at the information on the screen and assured Del that the entire program would be playing.

"Oh Jeff," he sighed. He put his hands over his eyes and listened intently. His voice choked as he whispered, "I can remember sitting in the kitchen while my mother made dinner and this program played on the radio." He took his hands away and swept his sleeve across his eyes.

The show crackled in the background as Del fought to contain himself. The air was moist from the rain. A breeze cut through the room and brought a refreshing release.

"This is the exact program, isn't it?" Del asked. "It's not actors portraying the old show?"

"It's the exact show," I told him.

He took a deep breath and exhaled. "This is bringing back all of these memories I'd shut down and forgotten years ago. It's a little much for me to handle."

"We can turn it off and you can listen to it later," I explained to him.

We did that, and I bookmarked the series so that he could get back to it with ease. I showed him some other features of the system and made my way to the door.

"I'm sorry I lost my composure back there, but all these images started flying through my head and I couldn't control it. I haven't thought about my mother in years, and in an instant I felt like we had traveled back in time and landed right in my kitchen. She looked just like she had when I was eight years old. Thinking about that reminded me how much I missed her. She died the day before my fifty-second birthday."

I told Del I understood and let him know that he should call if he needed me to explain anything to him.

When I arrived home I had six e-mails from Del, all vulgar and offensive. I responded and checked in on my other messages. Just as I was logging off, another message from Del flashed to me.

"Dear FireCracker,
This is the greatest invention of our time. I can see that I'm going to get into some colossal trouble with this thing. Where's all the porn I've been hearing about?
Del"

47

Peppers

The truck was on its last legs. It was backfiring now if I pressed on the accelerator too quickly. Del loved it. He would chuckle and turn to me and smile every time it happened. If someone next to us in a car or on the street flinched or ducked, Del would erupt into hysterical laughter.

We stopped by ImprovOlympic so that Del could pick up his check, and then we headed to the bank. Before he jumped into the truck, he stopped momentarily. He looked at the plastic on the window and asked me, "Can we take this truck on Lake Shore Drive?"

"It's illegal, but we could do it," I informed him.

He pulled back the tape and rolled down the plastic sheet carefully so that we could reattach it later. He put the plastic on the floor beneath his feet and settled into his seat.

"Will you take me onto Lake Shore Drive?" he asked. "The leaves are changing, and I want to see the colors along the lake."

I drove north and jumped onto the Drive at Irving Park, heading south. I rolled down my window so that the crisp wind would flow through the entire cab.

"Take it as slow as you can legally go," he sighed as he sat forward and chewed on his lip.

I kept the pace at a steady thirty-five miles an hour. That was the minimum speed on the Drive. Below that, we would be breaking the law—which we were already violating by driving a pickup truck on Lake Shore Drive. I wanted to abide by some rules.

Traffic was light in mid-afternoon. If anyone minded that we were there, they didn't show it. We puttered along with an occasional backfire, but no one paid us any notice.

I slid off the Drive near Navy Pier at Grand Avenue. I asked Del if he wanted me to turn around and drive back the other way.

"Nope," he said. "That'll do me until I die. Let's eat."

Del's new food obsession was stir-fry. We deposited his check at the bank and drove to a nearby restaurant. He loved the novelty of the Big Bowl because it allowed customers to pick the items for the stir-fry and then watch it be cooked, or they could return to their seats and it would be delivered to them.

In the area along North Michigan Avenue it was difficult to find parking at any time of day. Del decided it would be great fun to have the valets park the beat-up truck, so he forked over fifteen bucks to have an attendant in a red blazer find a cushy spot right next to a brand-new oversized Chevy Suburban. The truck backfired as the valet nestled it into its parking spot. The kid flinched and ducked behind the steering wheel.

Del clapped his hands with glee. "Well worth the fifteen dollars," he chortled.

For some reason, Del liked to order my food for me. If it was a place I'd never been or neither of us had ever visited before, he would order both of us the same item. He would ask me what I thought looked good on the menu, and then he'd make a decision for both of us.

There were always reasons why he ordered food for me. Most of the time it was because he wanted me to try his favorite item on the menu. He would build it up so much that he would get hungry for it and order the same thing. Other times he wanted us both to try the specialty of the house. Often he did it because he thought I was too picky. It would drive him crazy how unimaginative I was when it came to food.

We walked through a line and put our vegetables in a bowl. Del informed the cooks that we would both be having the Kung-Pao chicken. At our table the server brought appetizers that Del had ordered.

As we munched on the calamari, Del confessed he had some things he wanted to talk about. "I discovered yesterday that there's an unusual situation with my health insurance," he told me. "I get my insurance through the Screen Actors Guild, but it expires at the end of January. I'm still going to get my insurance through SAG, but it will be a different insurance because I'll hit the mandatory retirement age on my birthday. So there's a month in between when my regular insurance stops and my retirement insurance kicks in."

"Can you get a waiver?" I asked him.

He explained that he was trying to get one, but he wasn't optimistic about it. Medicating Del was a little different than medicating most people. He had taken so many illegal drugs through the years that his body had built up a tolerance. He required heavy doses of everything. He told me that he had made an inventory: his monthly prescriptions totaled more than a thousand dollars without insurance.

Our food was arrived, and we alternated between the stir-fry and the calamari.

There wasn't an answer to Del's insurance problems. Looking at it from every angle, there was no way to solve it. There were thirty days he wouldn't be covered.

His medication could be taken care of as long as he visited the doctor just before his insurance expired. The concern was with the expected. While Del and Charna could schedule doc-tor visits and address drug timetables, there was no solution for a sudden illness or unanticipated physical ailment. It seemed unimaginable that Del could go for a month without visiting a physician. His body had been breaking down steadily in recent years, and unexpected ailments were popping up frequently.

"Why couldn't this have happened in June or July? Nobody gets sick then. Of course it has to happen in fucking February in Chicago," he moaned.

I shuddered at the thought. The entire city of Chicago spent most of the month of February nursing sore throats and sniffles. That seemingly minor affliction would be debilitating to Del. He wouldn't be able to treat it with over-the-counter drugs. It would be necessary to get him to a physician, and the costs would escalate from there. Charna would spare no expense in making sure that Del's health was cared for, but he didn't want to rely on that. He never wanted to be someone else's burden.

We decided we had exhausted the subject of health insur-ance, so our thoughts turned to the previous evening's UCB show. As Del discussed his favorite scene, I picked at my food. I was pretty full and didn't want much more, but I took a bite occasionally. I noticed the hard shell of a blackened chili pep-per on my plate and held it up for Del to see.

"I didn't eat these. Are we supposed to eat them?" I asked.

"I ate mine," he said and returned to talking about UCB.

I popped the pepper into my mouth and bit into it. There was a four-second delay before I felt an explosion on my tongue. The pepper was so hot I thought it had burned a hole in the top of my mouth. I grabbed my napkin and tried to spit the pepper into it. I couldn't form any saliva, and I couldn't get the pepper out with my fingers. I shoved the napkin inside my mouth and tried to scrape the pepper out.

Del was oblivious to all of this. He continued to eat and prattle on about his students' TV show.

A drink of water momentarily relieved the fire in my mouth, but then it actually spread the inflammation around. Most servers at restaurants that specialize in spicy food will tell you that cold drinks compound the problem. The burning feeling in the mouth will be doused with foods of about the same temperature or warm drinks.

Del looked up at me. I had tears in my eyes. "Jesus. What now?" he asked dourly.

I had a problem getting words to come out. I finally managed to stutter, "I have to go to the bathroom."

"Go," he said ruefully.

As I walked away from the table, Del barked out, "We are never going to eat out again!"

I stumbled into the restroom and put my head under the faucet. Sweat and tears were pouring down my face. People walked in to use the facilities, but I could have cared less. I wadded up a paper towel and soaked it in cold water in the sink. I stuffed the entire paper towel in my mouth and sat on the floor. I put my face against the tiled wall and relished its coldness.

As the burning subsided, I returned to the table. I looked at my watch. I had been in the bathroom for fifteen minutes.

Del was eating the rest of my food as I settled into my seat. "I assume you don't want any more of this," he said, shoveling my abandoned food into his mouth. I didn't trust that I could speak without choking, so I just nodded.

"What did you eat?" he asked.

I pointed at a blackened chili pepper, and Del scooped it into his mouth. He bit into it and immediately spat it back onto the plate.

"Jesus Fucking Christ in Heaven!" he exclaimed banging his fist against the table.

"I told you," I said back to him.

"I thought I'd eaten one already. I guess I hadn't. Holy shit. It's like something just bit off the end of my tongue." He took heavy breaths and sweat started to form on his forehead.

Our server walked over and gave us some hot tea. "Drink this," she said as she placed a couple of cups in front of us. She stood beside Del for a while and instructed him to eat some of the calamari.

Del excused himself from the table and headed to the men's room. While he was away, I paid the bill and had the server box up his leftovers.

Del returned to the table ten minutes later with the front of his shirt soaked with water. My shirt was equally drenched. I commented, "The rest of the people in the restaurant think there's a pool in the basement."

We stood outside and waited for the truck to be brought around.

"We're idiots." I said to Del.

"Yes, we are," he replied.

The valet pulled the truck around to the front of the restaurant. It backfired as he stopped.

48

Impounded

Because the gas gauge on the truck hadn't worked in a while, I had developed a rhythm for getting gas. Every fifty miles I put ten dollars' worth of gas in the tank. I told Del we were low, but he wanted me to wait to buy gas near his house.

Meanwhile he had me driving all over the city looking for a book that we couldn't find in any normal bookstore. There was one store in Old Town that Del had never ever visited, so we inched along toward North Avenue. I could feel the truck struggling and warned Del that it was dying. The steering wheel jerked in my hands as the truck lurched forward and stalled. It died on a side road a few blocks from the bookstore; I coasted into a parking spot on the street.

Del walked to the bookstore while I walked to a nearby gas station. They had no gas can I could buy, so I walked a few blocks further to another station with a convenience store attached. They did have gas cans—at fifteen dollars a piece. I walked back to the bookstore and filled Del in on the situation.

Del had a gas can at his apartment, he said. He talked me into waiting and going to his place to get it, then taking a cab back. I took that to mean that we were going to Del's place immediately. We were not.

We would not leave the bookstore for another two hours. By the time we arrived at Del's apartment, it was 7:15. I had a Deep Schwa show at 8:00 and had to get to ImprovOlympic.

Del wanted to return to the bookshop in Old Town and sell them some of his old books, so we decided that I'd meet him the next day. We'd return to Old Town with a gas can and some old books.

But the next day, my truck was gone. We walked around for an hour looking for it, but it was nowhere to be found.

Del went back into the bookshop while I went to a pay phone. I dialed 311, the city's information number. I was then transferred to the Department of Revenue, where I was informed that my truck had been considered abandoned and a hazard, so it had been towed to a city lot.

"Why don't we just have me buy you a new car?" Del responded when I told him we had to go to Forty-seventh and Kedzie to retrieve the truck.

"Why?" I asked.

"I'd rather give you four thousand dollars to buy a car than go through the shit that we're going to have to deal with," he replied.

I should have taken his money. We were at the tow lot for five hours.

To get the truck we had to have the title and proof of insurance, both of which were in the vehicle. I was not allowed to get the items from the truck until I could prove that I was the rightful owner. The original title was at my parents' home in Bethany, Illinois. I phoned them, and they faxed the title to a currency exchange a few blocks away. We had the fax notarized and returned to wait in line once more.

We were fourteenth in line to get to the window. Two people in front of us were taken away by security for threatening the highly irritable workers at the window. Every conversation before ours started at a normal level and escalated to a loud, heated exchange. Ours was no different.

"Listen you cocksucker, you have all our information, now give us our car!" Del screamed at the woman behind the glass.

I tried to calm him down, but it was difficult because I was just as angry. The woman behind the glass was hostile and aggressive and had yet to speak to us in a civil tone.

"Before I can let you get your car, I have to have a photocopy of your driver's license," she shouted at Del.

Del screamed back at her, "He just handed you his fucking license!"

"I said, he has to give me a *photocopy* of his license. Not his actual license."

I thought Del was about to go through the glass. His face was red with fury, and he was spitting as he roared at her.

"There's a goddamn photocopier right behind you. Turn your fat ass around and photocopy his license."

"It's not our job to make photocopies of your goddamn license," she bellowed at us. "Go get a photocopy and get back in line and we'll see if I let you in to get your car."

It was exasperating. We went back to the currency exchange and copied the license. Del stayed outside while I stood in line to get permission to get into the lot to try to get the title and insurance papers. I walked to the truck, brought back the information, and stood in line again. Now there was another problem: the registration sticker had expired. I called my parents again. They looked through the mail and discovered that the sticker had been mailed to them. They'd mail it to me, but it wouldn't come for a few days.

When I stepped outside, Del was standing with a tow-truck driver. It turned out that the driver could tow my truck off the lot. Del gave the driver some money, and we sat on a couple of old tires and waited. Two hours later the tow-truck driver received clearance to tow my Ford Ranger out.

"I wish we had just bought you a new car," Del cackled.

"This has been one of the most frustrating experiences I've ever been through," I lamented to him.

"This seems like an odd thing to say right now, but I really enjoy these little excursions of ours," Del said to me with a smile.

I looked at him with a surprised look on my face. It sounded like he was making a joke, but I could tell he was sincere. "This was awful, Del," I told him.

"It was terrible, but it was fun and exciting."

"What are you talking about?" I said with disbelief.

"I always preach that there are two types of scenes in improv," Del said. "There are 'Slice of Life' scenes and then there are 'The Day Something Happens' scenes. In 'Slice of Life' scenes we see the normal routine of normal people and watch how they operate in a slice of their day. In 'The Day Something Happens' we see the same normal people in the same routine, but today a decision has been made that alters how they exist. It feels like the last few years I've settled into a 'Slice of Life' routine. These trips with you have launched me back into 'The Day Something Happens'—and for that I thank you, Firecracker."

"I'd rather settle back into the boring 'Slice of Life' routine," I admitted.

"Not me," Del answered. "I love it. When was the last chance I had to scream 'cocksucker' at someone in a crowded room?"

When the truck arrived, we both thought the driver had brought us the wrong vehicle. The driver's side window was now busted out, and there were cracks in the windshield. Since I had visited the truck to get the license and insurance, the car had been severely abused. There were dents all over the body, and the flatbed was filled with rocks and cinder blocks.

I now stood in line for another thirty minutes to fill out a form stating that my vehicle had been damaged during its stay in the impound lot. City employees stepped outside and inspected the truck. As I was using Del's can to put fuel in the gas tank, the pound inspector determined that my claim would be denied. He handed Del another form and walked back into the building.

I had reached the end of my rope and was ready to call it quits. Brushing the glass out of the seat, I started the truck. Del tossed the form onto the front seat and walked back toward the building. "Del," I shouted. "Come back."

He was on a mission, but I had no idea what he was going to do. He knocked on the window and stood there. People started yelling, and I could see some people grabbing phones. Del was peeing on the building. He turned around, zipped up his pants, and ran toward the truck.

"We can't leave normally, can we?" I said to Del.

He shrugged and giggled. "Just keep driving, and don't stop."

"Del," I reminded him. "We need gas."

"Oh my God," he remembered. "I probably shouldn't have done that," he laughed.

I looked at him and started laughing too.

"Let's see how far we can go."

49

Illegal U-turns

Del decided he wanted to buy Charna a Web-TV system. He enjoyed his so much that he wanted to give it to her as an early Christmas present. Del was agnostic and Charna was Jewish, but they both celebrated the Christmas holiday. We had purchased the system just before Thanksgiving. Del had given it to her, but it wasn't working properly. We decided we would forgo our usual errands to go to Charna's so I could figure out what the problem was.

"Of course the system I gave Charna is broken," Del sighed. "I could give a hundred of these things to a hundred different people, but Charna's is always going to be the one that's broken."

As soon as we arrived, Charna immediately brought us popsicles and sodas. I felt like a kid again. It was surreal watching Del suck on a popsicle while sitting on Charna's bed.

I tried several ways to get Charna's Web-TV to work, but it was useless. There was no way I was going to get it up and running. I sat on the floor in the middle of Charna's bedroom working on the system while her dog Gracie sat beside me with her chin in my lap.

The previous day I had taken a trip to Milwaukee with my friend Jackie. She had driven there for an audition; I went along because I'd never visited Milwaukee before. When I told Del and Charna about the trip, they waxed on about their visits to the Wisconsin city while I packed up the Web-TV and prepared to take back to Best Buy to exchange it.

It was a December afternoon, but the temperature was in the sixties. We drove in Charna's convertible with the top down. It felt like the world was moving in slow motion as the three of us made our way south on Ashland toward Clybourn. The sky was bright blue. Del kept turning around from the front seat and smiling.

"I could do this all day. This is great," Del said as his hair bristled in the wind. "We should go eat and see a movie."

When we arrived at the electronics store, Del grabbed my arm as we climbed out of the car. "She's going to yell and scream because she lost the receipt. I'm not going to be anywhere around when that happens, so you'll have to come and get me when it's all finished."

I had no idea they didn't have the receipt. This was going to get ugly.

We walked in together. Immediately the clerk asked for Charna's receipt. She started yelling about the fact that the Web-TV system didn't work and had never worked. In her defense, her hearing is not the best. She often doesn't realize that she's yelling.

"That was fast," I turned to say to Del, but he was gone. I saw him hurrying down the main aisle. He never looked back.

Charna continued talking to the Best Buy employee as I dutifully stood beside her. At one point the employee turned to me and said, "You can understand, sir, that we can't credit the return unless there's a receipt. We don't even really know if this system was bought here."

I shrugged my shoulders and said, "Don't tell me, I'm just her little retarded friend." Both looked at me like I was insane, and they continued arguing.

Two hours later we left Best Buy with a new Web-TV. Serial numbers were checked and a great deal of paperwork was filed.

It was now almost six o'clock. I hadn't thought the excursion would take so long, so I had volunteered to work that evening, to give a nighttime tour. I was supposed to clock-in at seven. I started to get antsy.

Charna's new system worked perfectly on the first attempt. She invited both of us to dinner, and Del decided to stay. I explained that I had to give a tour. Charna gave me a popsicle as I left.

"This was a pretty fun day," Del said as I headed out the door.

"For the first time, neither of us were the people that started the ruckus," I laughed.

I raced to my apartment and grabbed my tour guide uniform—a pair of khaki pants and a green polo shirt. I had half an hour to get to Eighteenth and Indiana, and it appeared I would make it easily.

In my head I pictured Del, Charna, and I driving in Charna's car. Everything seemed perfect—the three of us smiling and laughing as Del tried to talk us into going to see the dinosaur movie at the Imax.

My mind turned back to driving as I approached the intersection of Clark and Belmont. Heading south, I watched as a woman in a brand new Chrysler Le Baron began to pull out of her parking spot and ease into traffic. I noticed that her attention was concentrated on oncoming traffic; she never once looked at what was coming from behind her. She gradually slid the nose of her car farther into the southbound lane as I approached. I honked my horn just as she pushed on the accelerator and slammed into the front of my truck. She intended to make a U-turn; she never saw me coming.

As I pulled forward and inched ahead, I heard an awful screeching noise. I got out of the car and felt my head. I had slammed it into the steering wheel and could feel a bump starting to grow.

I looked at the truck. The right tire rod was bent, and the right front end was demolished. I called work to tell them I didn't think I was going to make it. The woman and I waited for the police to arrive and, after a few hours, they eventually did. Thankfully, two Dunkin' Donuts employees who were outside on a smoke break witnessed the entire event. After they told the officers what they had seen, the woman was given a ticket for the accident.

I tried to drive the truck to work to put in as many hours as possible, but it stopped dead at Eighteenth and State. It had taken an hour to make it that far. I popped the hood and could see that the engine was pretty mangled. A puddle began forming under the truck. I had been leaking gas ever since leaving the accident scene.

I jumped on the Red Line train and went back home to my apartment. I called Del as soon as I had settled in.

"Oh no!" he exclaimed. "Is the truck okay?"

"Thanks for asking if I'm all right."

"I loved that truck," he reminded me. "I could give two shits about you."

I told Del the truck had met its demise and could not be salvaged. He talked for a while about the good times we had had in the truck before eventually asking about my health. I told him I had a bump on my head and I was a little sore, but I was okay.

A few minutes later Charna called to say that she was picking me up to take me to the hospital. I told her that wasn't necessary. I promised to have my roommate, Mike, call her if I had any problems.

Before I went to bed I checked my e-mail. There was a message from Del:

"Firecracker,

Do you think there's a way we could arrange a burial at sea for the truck? I truly loved that magnificent piece of mangled metal.

Let's not dilly-dally around. Let me buy you a new car in appreciation for your work and your friendship this last year. I joked around about it, but I would have been devastated if anything had happened to you. I've grown to become pretty fond of you, you fucking little retard.

I can't believe the truck is dead. Surely I'm next.

Del"

50

Blizzards of All Kinds

I went several weeks without seeing Del. We conversed through e-mail, but without a vehicle we couldn't make our weekly trips. Each day Del sent me an e-mail with pictures of cars he thought he should buy for me. I would respond that I was saving money and would buy a car soon. I considered borrowing cars, as I had done when I first started driving him around, but Del assured me that it wasn't that urgent yet.

His constant offers to buy me a car were tempting. I explained to him that I couldn't accept a gift of such enormity. Del modified his offer so that the car would act as payment for services rendered, or so that the money for it would be a loan I wouldn't have to pay back until 2018.

Two days after 1999 was ushered in, Chicago was hit with the second-worst blizzard in the city's history. Twenty-two inches of snow accumulated in three days. Everything in the city closed down, including museums and public transportation.

On January 3, while the city was virtually shut down, Del called me and insisted I come to his apartment. He sounded pretty panicked, so I bundled up and walked the mile and a half to his place. A walk that normally takes fifteen minutes took more than an hour.

I arrived at Del's place and accepted the ritual cup of tea. I didn't even check to make sure the cup was clean or the bag was unused. I was tired and cold and needed something warm.

He looked like he hadn't slept in days. His apartment was cleaner than the last time I had visited. It wasn't immaculate by any means, but it was certainly neater than normal.

"Who cleaned up?" I asked him as I let the steam from the mug settle against my face.

"I did," he responded.

"What's going on?"

"I need your help," he said as he began to bite his lip.

I drank my tea and waited for an explanation. Del stood up and walked into his front room. He carried a few boxes into his living room and motioned for me to join him. I sat on the couch and waited for him to give me orders.

"I was having problems sleeping last night, and I realized the government could very easily come into this apartment after I die and make a clean sweep of everything. No one would know that I ever existed."

I tried to comprehend what he was asking me to do.

"In these boxes are all my newspaper clippings and all the important documents of my life. We need to go through everything and decide what you're going to take home with you."

"Take home with me?" I asked.

"Yes," he answered. "I need you to keep some things for me."

I knew there was no way to change his mind, but I felt the need to reassure him. "Del, the government is not going to erase your existence."

Sitting beside him was a small magazine. Del tossed it to me. The title was *National Alliance*. It was an anti-government magazine that leaned toward racial segregation.

"Why do you have this?" I asked him.

He shrugged. "After Ruby Ridge and the Oklahoma City bombing, I was curious about what motivated these people, so I sent for a copy of their newsletter. Now I seem to be on their mailing lists."

"Tell them to stop sending this crap to you," I told him.

On the second page of *National Alliance* was an article about an entire family that had disappeared. The author of the article believed the government had managed to convince everyone that the family had never existed. I looked at Del and saw that this was what had sparked his paranoia.

"There's another incident just like that in this magazine," Del said, handing me another magazine called *American Renaissance.*

"How many of these things do you have?" I asked him.

"I don't know. They're pretty tenacious. When it comes to propaganda, they're worse than the Christians, and I didn't think anyone was worse than the Christians."

He began to rummage through the boxes and indicated I should start looking as well. "Once I'm gone, everything can be easily removed. No one will remember I was ever here," he said. "Not immediately, but eventually, I'll be reduced to folklore or a fable or, God forbid, an anecdote."

I picked up a picture. It was of Del as a child pointing a toy gun at the camera. At least it looked like a toy gun. With Del you didn't always know. A four-year-old Del holding a real gun would explain a lot.

We spent the better part of the next four hours looking through boxes. We set aside reviews and articles Del was especially proud of, and collected all the legal documents we could find—his birth certificate, his parents' marriage license, and several film and television contracts were all placed in a large envelope. After a great deal of thought, Del decided to put several letters he had written to his mother inside the envelope.

Until that afternoon I hadn't realized Del had kept in touch with his mother. The two of them had conversed and corresponded routinely through the years until her death. He sent her all his press clippings; she sent him poetry she had written.

"I started my little poetry magazine when I was in middle school because I knew she would be proud of that," he told me as the snow continued to fall and accumulate outside the window. It was dark outside. I had been in his apartment for several hours. I was dreading the long walk home.

We took several pictures out of the box and put them in the envelope. Once we were satisfied we had gathered enough information, Del would find another box and we would add a few more articles and a few more reviews to the mix.

My stomach began growling from hunger. Del heard this and produced some bread and lunch meat from his refrigerator. I was skeptical at first but eventually caved and ate two sandwiches.

"I think we've got enough," I told him as I double-checked the contents of the envelope.

He had calmed down quite a bit and seemed relieved. He held the envelope as I climbed back into all the different layers of my winter clothing.

Del put his hand on my shoulder as I reached for the envelope and took what he believed to be the most important documents of his life. I felt like I had done the right thing. I didn't believe for an instant there was a government organization that went around erasing people's histories, but it was useless to try to change his mind. I also knew there were several layers to Del's paranoia. It was possible he didn't realize it was more than just the government he was worried about.

I turned and opened the door and started down the stairs. Looking out the window on the stairwell I could see that mounds of snow had risen.

"Firecracker," Del said as I descended the stairs. I turned and could see the concern in his face. "I existed. If they forget, tell them."

51

The New Car

Spoo had been doing well and had managed to persuade the *Chicago Sun-Times* to send a reviewer to the show.
She liked it. Del was ecstatic to have two well-reviewed shows
on Saturday nights. The Lindbergh Babies were the most popular and most respected, but we held our own.

For the most part, the Lindbergh Babies despised Spoo.
They felt our form was elementary and amateurish, and they
openly mocked our "Hymns of Praise" that we used to begin
each show. Like a Greek chorus, we would proclaim these
hymns based on suggestions from the audience.

It was understandable. The Lindbergh Babies' form was designed to showcase their intelligence, and their scenes epito-
mized the smart, slow work that Del taught. Spoo's form was
simplistic. We had a problem, though: the audience kept giving
us the suggestion of "toothbrush." In eighteen months we had
twenty shows based on "toothbrush."

Del called me the Firecracker because he felt I played with
an urgency that made everyone seem imperative and com-
pelling. He designed our show to highlight that type of imme-
diacy in our scenes.

"Start every scene in the middle," he instructed. Unfortunately we didn't always succeed, and our failures were magnified because unsuccessful urgency came off as "jokey."

Yet our successes far outweighed our defeats. Del enjoyed Spoo, so much so that he encouraged us to apply to the Big Stinkin' Improv Festival in Austin. He was again scheduled to teach there and felt we would serve as a good example of the things he planned to present.

"The organizers of the festival have assured me that Spoo will be given a prime-time slot when we go down there," Del told us as we gathered in the green room after one of our shows. It was a bitterly cold February evening, and we had been surprised to see Del at the show. He came to see us almost every Saturday night but had missed the last few weeks because of the weather. I also knew he was being extra cautious because he was in the middle of that thirty-day period without health insurance.

"I really enjoy this group, and I think people deserve to see it. I also think you all deserve the attention of having a national stage to present this little piece we've put together," he said before launching into one of his famous coughing fits.

We talked about ideas for fund-raisers and, after a brief discussion, adjourned the meeting. As the room cleared, Del motioned to me that he had another matter to discuss.

As he approached, I smiled. "I bought a car," I said.

His face lit up.

"We can get back to our weekly errands on Thursday," I told him.

"That's great," he said. "It'll be good to get back into that routine again." As an afterthought he added, "What happened to the truck?"

I knew how much he loved the truck, so I regretted telling him about it. "The woman's insurance company came and took it. They put it in the compactor and destroyed it."

"Jesus," he replied wistfully. "Let's go to a Cubs game this summer and toss the remains of the truck onto the field." We both laughed hysterically. He grabbed onto the wall as he broke into another coughing fit. He seemed tired. His speech had slowed quite a bit.

"I've another matter to discuss with you," he informed me. "I've been conversing with a man in New York who has written a play about my escapades with Severn Darden. His theater company is going to pay to have me spend a couple of months in New York directing the show."

I was surprised and happy to hear this news. Del had regretted not doing *Death of a Salesman*, and while this new venture was on a smaller scale, it would certainly help him to get back to projects that expanded his world.

"I also told them I would be bringing someone with me," he continued. "I'd like for you to consider going to New York with me to play the part of Severn."

I had expected him to ask me to come and be his assistant. I hadn't expected the offer to become part of the production. He told me that he had arranged for the company to supply him with an assistant and that my sole responsibility would be to play a role in the performance.

"There's no need to answer now, because we're still in the negotiating phase, but I want you to consider it."

"I'll do it," I told him.

"Good," he answered. "I think it'll be a good time. I'll let you know when anything becomes official."

All the other people had left the room; Del and I were there alone. We talked for a little while about my new car, and he grew excited about having our weekly visits again. "No more visits to restaurants," he announced. "I've come to the realization that we're diner people."

I thought about Del and me in New York. "It would be nice to have a whole other city of people to torment," I told him.

"Let's try and take it easy in the new city. We always end up being more damaged than everyone else," he replied.

I asked if he wanted to stay and watch "Sex Wars." "No," he said. "I don't need to stay anymore. These things can all go on without me."

He put his hand on my shoulder and squeezed it. "It was good seeing you Jeff," he said, and walked out of the green room.

I gathered my things. It was the last conversation Del and I would have.

52

The Birthday Party

I called Del several times before Thursday. He didn't respond to my phone calls or e-mails.

Friday went by and still no response. Spoo had our usual show on Saturday, and I showed up to perform for the 10:30 show. Upon arriving, I was greeted by Jason Chin, director of the training center.

On the ramp that led down to the IO cabaret, Jason told me that Charna had taken Del to Illinois Masonic Hospital. He was in serious condition. Early reports from people who had visited Del were that he was in good humor but in fairly serious discomfort.

Several members of the Lindbergh Babies had visited Del at the hospital. He appeared to be in good spirits, they said, and was recuperating from complications of emphysema. They said he had laughed and joked around with everyone and really seemed to be doing well.

I talked to Charna when she stopped by the theater, and she brought me up to date on the situation. Brian Doyle Murray had called the hospital to talk to Del, she said. When Charna handed Del the phone, Brian started choking and gasping and shouting through the phone line, "Help! Help! I'm dying." Del laughed and talked with him for a while.

Charna said she was optimistic. She encouraged me to visit Del, and I told her I would try to stop by. In my mind, though, I didn't plan on going. I figured this was a temporary visit for Del. I would see him once he was home again. From the way everyone talked, I expected that would be soon.

When I arrived at ImprovOlympic for my Deep Schwa show the next day, the reports were grimmer. People were talking about the possibility of Del not being released from the hospital. Rumors began spreading that he would have to be placed in a nursing home or a clinic because the emphysema had so damaged his body that he would need constant attention and a respirator to help him breathe.

I knew that would never happen. Del and Charna had an agreement that if he ever had to rely on machines to remain alive, she would inject him with heroin and help him overdose. Del truly believed that Charna would follow through with the plan. So did Charna.

Monday morning at 5 a.m., Charna was called to the hospital. Del was fading. The doctors didn't think he would make it to the sunrise. She arrived to find him close to death. As she tells it, Del was unable to speak, so she gave him some paper and a pencil so he could communicate with her. His breathing slowed as he scrawled out the words, "I love you." He closed his eyes and Charna began to cry as she listened to the heart monitor slow to a steady hum. His heart had stopped. Del was dead.

In an instant, medical technicians swarmed the room. A tube was shoved down his throat to open his breathing airway. For several moments, they administered CPR until Del's heart began pumping once again. Within moments his eyes opened and he regained consciousness. He violently motioned for the doctors to take the tube out of his throat.

When the tube was out, Del screamed with all his power, "You motherfucking bastards! You robbed me of my right to die!"

Neither Charna nor Del was aware that they were required to sign a do-not-resuscitate agreement if they did not want him to be revived. Del was incensed that he had been cheated from death; Charna was exhausted at the idea of saying goodbye all over again and watching him die a second time.

The doctors informed Charna and Del that they did not expect him to make it through the week. They asked him if there was anything he wanted before he died. He told everyone that indeed he had some final wishes.

Both Jason Chin and Charna called to tell me that Del's final wish was to have a birthday party with all his former students. The party was to be held at the hospital. A notice was sent at once to everyone whom Del had taught to come to Chicago. He desperately wanted all his students there for one last party.

When I called the hospital and was transferred to Del's room, I asked to speak to Charna. She wasn't there. I told the person who had answered the phone my name and explained that I was one of Del's students and was looking for an update on his condition. To my surprise, she gave the phone directly to Del.

"Thanks for coming and visiting me, you little twit," he growled. His voice was scratchy and he spoke slowly, but he seemed pretty normal to me.

"I keep hearing that you're sick, but you seem pretty feisty to me," I told him.

"I'm faking it," he told me. "I'm pretty close to being dead."

"You always think you're dying," I teased him. "I don't believe any of this."

"I would think this would make you pretty happy, Fire-cracker," he said. "You've been trying to kill me for the past two years."

I laughed, and Del started coughing. After he settled himself he added, "Tell Charna that I want her to take some of my money and buy you a new truck. And I don't want you to get a used one. I want you to have a brand-new one."

I tried to tell Del that *he* should tell Charna, because she would never listen to me. Before I could get the entire sentence out, Del started coughing and eventually handed the phone back to his visitor. She encouraged me to come to Del's birthday party and hung up. I could hear Del coughing as the phone disconnected.

It all seemed to me ridiculously extravagant and unnecessary. Del had been sick and close to death before. There was no doubt in my mind that he would beat this one as well. He was being dramatic and trying hard to be the center of attention.

Before I made my way to the hospital for Del's birthday party, I stopped by the Jewel on Ashland and bought some pumpernickel and caviar. I didn't know if Del was in any condition to eat it, but I was sure it wouldn't go to waste.

I picked up Jason Chin and we drove to the hospital together. Jason was also the coach of Deep Schwa at the time, so we planned on attending the party for a couple of hours before making our way back to ImprovOlympic for that evening's show. We arrived at Illinois Masonic off North Halsted and followed the signs pointing us to the room where the party was scheduled.

In the party room it was difficult to navigate our way through the crowds of people. Celebrities and television cameras were everywhere. As I maneuvered my way, I suddenly felt silly. I knew very few people, and I was weaving between them carrying a loaf of bread and caviar.

It was loud in the room as people chatted freely. Some of Del's old students were talking with people they hadn't seen in years. I slid between two people and suddenly bumped into someone and dropped the bread. I bent down to pick it up, and as I popped back up I almost bumped into someone else. I felt a mixture of joy and surprise as I recognized I had just bumped into Bill Murray.

"I'm sorry," I managed.

"Don't worry about it, guy," he responded.

I had always worshiped Murray. That night's events solidified him for me as a wonderful all-around person. Del had always spoken fondly of him, and I had witnessed Del's side of phone calls with him on a few occasions. After he hung up the phone, Del once said to me, "If you were reincarnated and had to be reborn into mortality, the Dalai Lama would probably be the most desired embodiment to be reborn in. I'd imagine that coming back as Bill Murray would be second."

Bill had paid for all of the evening's festivities as a gift to Del. It was his way of showing respect for his former teacher.

In the center of the room, Del sat in a wheelchair. People surrounded him so that I didn't notice him at first. Jason walked up and said a few words and Del nodded. I walked up and put the bread and caviar on the tray beside him.

"Great fucking gift," Del said in a hoarse voice.

"You look great," I told him, and I really believed he did. He had tubes going into his nose to help him breathe, but he looked no different from the last time he and I had done our weekly errands. In fact he looked a little better than our last visit: they had bathed and groomed him to look cleaner than I had ever seen him.

Food was everywhere and people encouraged us to eat. A bartender made Del his favorite drink, a white chocolate martini, and Charna read telegrams from people around the country who couldn't attend. Howard Hesseman, Robin Williams, and Peter Boyle sent telegrams extending get-well wishes with birthday greetings. Wavy Gravy sent a four-word message that was short and to the point: "See you in hell."

A camera crew from Comedy Central taped the event and recorded a short interview with Del. Four actors from the Upright Citizens Brigade couldn't be there because they were filming their TV show, but they had Del give them instructions through the camera for a sketch they were producing in the upcoming months.

Meanwhile Del's former and present students continued to file into the party room. Celebrities milled throughout. Remarkably, this living wake was pretty festive. Morbid and unusual, but peculiarly jovial.

"I think he needs a little encouragement, I think that's all he needs," Bill Murray said as he was being interviewed by a *Sun-Times* reporter. "Whatever he's going to do next, whatever his next project is."

Just a few feet away, director Harold Ramis was speaking to a *Chicago Tribune* reporter. "Del was—is—the single most powerful force in improv comedy in America," Ramis told the reporter.

Out of the corner of my eye I saw an interesting-looking man and woman make their way into the room. They were wearing ceremonial gowns. Charna introduced them as a Wiccan high priest and high priestess. Del had asked for a Wiccan religious ceremony to be performed at the party. They chanted and conducted a ceremony that was foreign to me but made Del immensely happy.

When the ceremony ended, Del spoke to the crowd. "I guess I better die now. Otherwise a lot of people are going to be pretty disappointed," he announced. He spoke about his joy of teaching and thanked everyone for participating in what he felt had been a truly magnificent adventure.

Bernie Sahlins approached Del's wheelchair to say a final farewell. The two men had rarely spoken since Del had left Second City. The battle over improv as an art form had driven a wedge between them. In 1985 Bernie had sold his shares of Second City to Andrew Alexander and Len Stuart. As Bernie wished him well, Del held up his finger and leaned forward. "It is an art form," Del said with a growl. Bernie chuckled, relinquishing the battle that had nagged at them for many years. "Del, for tonight it is an art form," Bernie responded. It appeared as if Del was chuckling along with him until someone nudged Bernie and said, "Bernie, you're standing on his air tube."

Jason and I witnessed this exchange as we stood behind Bernie waiting to talk with Del. We had to leave to get to our show. We went to Del and said our goodbyes.

"Come and visit," he told me as I put my hand on his shoulder.

I assured him that I would visit him soon and that I would definitely make it on his birthday.

"Tomorrow," he whispered. "You better try and make it tomorrow."

I promised I would come the next day, and then I struggled to get to the lobby and out to the street. We drove to the theater just in time for me to make my way to the stage. Everyone at the theater asked about Del's condition.

"He looks great. He spoke and he was very funny. He doesn't look like a man who's dying. He just looks like he's sick," I told everyone.

After a moment of thought, I added, "He'll be back teaching in no time. I'd be shocked if he doesn't pull out of it soon."

53

Pitiful

I arrived at Illinois Masonic Hospital and received a guest pass to visit Del's room. I was not prepared for what I saw.

The previous night Del had been the epitome of dignity and grace. He had put on a brave face and performed a masterpiece to all who had seen him. Now, away from the eyes of the celebrities, his concerned students, and the collection of cameras, Del was a man in a great deal of pain. And he was dying.

I heard his groans before I walked into the room. When I entered and saw Del, my heart dropped to my stomach. He lay on his bed in the middle of the room, surrounded by flowers. He had a grimace on his face as he moaned and begged to be put out of his pain.

"Do something please," he cried out. "This is unbearable."

I stopped momentarily and considered leaving. I didn't want to see him like this. Charna saw me standing in the doorway and waved me in. My escape was thwarted.

Two of Del's former students were there with Charna. She bent down within a few inches of his face and told Del I had arrived.

"Firecracker?" he asked, but she didn't understand. She told him again that I was there, and he waved me over. As the nurse took Charna out to the hallway to talk to a doctor, I walked up to Del's bed. Del reached up and grabbed my shirt and pulled me closer to him.

"Thank God you're here. You've been dying to kill me, and now's your chance. Don't botch it this time," he choked out.

Everyone in the room chuckled at Del's joke and assured him I wasn't trying to kill him.

"He's an assassin, let him kill me," he pleaded with everyone.

"He's a little delirious sometimes," one of his students assured me.

"He's not delirious. He sincerely thinks I'm an assassin," I told the student. The student nodded but seemed annoyed that he didn't understand the joke. I was pleased that even as he was dying, Del was still helping me alienate people.

The doctor entered the room and talked to Del and Charna. The drugs they were giving Del weren't having any effect on him. Years of abuse had caused him to build up a tolerance to the drugs they were administering. The doctor told Del they were going to increase his dosage to try to ease his pain.

Charna and the doctor left the room to take care of paperwork. Del motioned for me to lean in so that he could talk. "This hurts so much. I never thought dying would hurt so much."

The student leaned in and tried to console Del, "Don't worry, Del, the doctors are going to get you fixed up. You'll be feeling better in no time."

Del glanced for a moment at the student and returned his gaze to me. "What a fucking idiot."

I laughed, and the student sat back in his seat annoyed at both of us.

"I didn't want to die like this. I wanted to die in a drug overdose or shot by a jealous husband because I fucked his wife," he lamented to me.

"I can see if there's someone here from the Make a Wish Foundation. Maybe we can have them arrange to send a horny housewife in here for you," I told him.

He laughed and started coughing. Once he stopped coughing he moaned, "I couldn't get a three of diamonds right now."

"It's a hospital, Del," I told him. "They have things they can give you that will give you an Ace of Spades."

Del started laughing again and moaned in pain.

"Maybe it would be best if you stopped making him laugh," the student told me.

Del barked back, "Maybe you should stop being a fucking douche bag." Every sentence Del spoke seemed to pain him. It was excruciating to watch him choke out the words. But that last sentence harked back to vintage Del: loud, boisterous, and scary.

"What day is it?" Del asked me. When I told him it was the fourth of March, he nodded.

"I thought so," he responded. "Tomorrow is the fifteenth anniversary of John Belushi's death. Monday's the anniversary of my mother's death."

After the doctor reentered with Charna, Del's morphine dosage was increased. Charna spoke to Del and told him that the additional dosage would cause him to drift in and out of consciousness. Del assured her that he didn't care how much they gave him—he just wanted the pain to stop. The doctor administered the morphine and told Charna he would return in half an hour.

While this conversation was going on, Miles Stroth, another of Del's former students, entered the room. It was apparent that he was surprised by Del's condition.

"Take me to your house, Charna," Del pleaded. "I don't want to die in a goddamn hospital. It's so cliché."

Charna assured him she would try to arrange it. She immediately left to speak to a nurse. I was impressed to see that she was actually making an attempt to move Del to her home. I had thought she was just trying to pacify him, but she wasn't.

Del's groans were becoming louder and longer. When a nurse asked him if his pain had subsided at all, he cried out in anguish. She told him that she had been directed to increase the dosage every hour until he became comfortable. He was on a morphine drip, and he begged her to increase the morphine. With the doctor's approval, she did.

After the nurse left, Del motioned for Miles and I to approach the bed. "I'm just so uncomfortable in this position. Move me."

Miles and I reached underneath Del and tried to shift him to a better position. He weighed over two hundred pounds and really wasn't able to help us in any way. He screamed as we moved him but urged us to continue. We set him down and stepped back.

Del was aghast. "You made it worse. This is awful."

The nurse entered the room, and Del asked her to move him. All by herself she maneuvered him to an ideal posture. Del thanked her and then looked at me with disgust. "Pitiful," he said, and shook his head.

He sighed and closed his eyes, and slipped into a restful sleep. Miles, the student, and I sat and watched Del sleep. There was an uncomfortable silence as we wondered if he had fallen asleep or perhaps had just died.

Miles sat on the other side of the room and somberly looked out the window. The student and I sat beside each other next to Del's bed.

"What if that was it?" I asked the student. "What if his last word was 'pitiful' because he was annoyed at us?"

Suddenly Del awoke and screamed out in pain, shocking all of us. "That was like a horror movie," I told Del, but he had no comprehension of what I was talking about.

He stayed alert and awake and asked me to tell him about Saturday's show with Spoo and the Lindbergh Babies. I filled him in on the scenes while he listened as best he could. It was apparent the current dosage wasn't helping.

Charna and the doctor returned, and Del begged them to increase the increments of morphine they were giving him. The doctor told Del and Charna that increasing the morphine would not be lethal but would allow him to be comfortable. But he wanted to make sure they both understood that the increased dosage could cause him to lose consciousness—and he might not wake up. Del told the doctor he understood. He just wanted to drift away in his sleep. He didn't want to die crying and screaming.

The dosage was increased and the doctor left.

I suddenly felt a tightness in my chest. I had spent the past year and a half with Del, and this was the first time I realized he was actually going to die. We had talked about it and joked about it, and there were times with him when I had thought he had died right in front of me. But it never seemed like it would ever really happen.

I stared at him as he grimaced and cried out in pain. It hit me that this was the last time I would see him alive. My throat felt like it was closing, and I was dizzy. Del wheezed as he breathed, and I could feel my breathing pattern match his. I didn't know what to do. I was standing there watching him die, and I felt helpless and useless.

Tears filled my eyes. I took a deep breath so that I could try to maintain my composure. My hands started to sweat as I gritted my teeth. I didn't want to watch him drift away. I needed to leave.

I walked to the side of the bed and told Del I was leaving. He was drifting in and out of consciousness, but he took my hand and urged me to move in closer.

"Don't try to kiss me," I joked to him and he smiled.

"You're a good friend," he whispered to me.

"I'll miss you, Grandpa," I said as strongly as I could.

"Goodbye, retard," he managed to say with a smile.

He was having difficulty keeping his eyes open. They closed, and it seemed like he had drifted back to sleep. I moved to say goodbye to Charna when suddenly Del gripped my hand. "Don't ever think this journey is about you. It's about everyone around you."

His hand loosened and he drifted off to sleep.

I said goodbye to Charna and walked to the doorway of the room. Del opened his eyes. I could see him talking with Charna, but the only thing I could hear was Del saying, "Thank God. I'm tired of being the funniest person in the room."

I turned and walked through the halls of the hospital. As I started my car and drove away from the hospital, I remembered a monologue that Del had written for "My Talk Show." As Ozzie Mandeus, Del had stared into the camera and recited:

"I was reading in a newspaper the other day about a sky-diver who dived out of an airplane and did aerial acrobatics for several thousand feet. When he pulled the ripcord, the main chute did not open. And then what did he do? He did flips and acrobatics head over heels at the top of his ability all the way into the ground. Splat. Now that's my kind of guy. That's kind of a metaphor for life, isn't it? I mean, we're all going to hit the ground—splat—eventually, aren't we? So what I'm going to do is follow that guy's example and do acrobatics all the way out."

Thirty minutes after I left the hospital, Del's heart stopped and he was pronounced dead. Charna and a few of his former students who had stopped by the hospital surrounded him and watched as he slipped away.

I was at home watching an episode of "South Park" Del had lent me.

Epilogue

by Charna Halpern

On the afternoon of March 4th, Del requested the morphine drip he had been promised to make his last hours more comfortable. I sat on his bed and held his hand while we waited for the technicians to bring the morphine to the room. "Promise me you'll make the skull thing happen. No matter what," he said. "I promise," I said. "And keep my ashes in the theater where I can affect the work." "I will," I promised. "And tell them all that we succeeded where others have failed. We created a theater of the heart—a theater where people cherish each other to succeed on stage. Tell the students 'theater of the heart.'" I cried at the beauty of what he had said. He was in great pain in his final hour, but still he concentrated on the importance of our work together. I witnessed absolutely no fear in him when he faced his death, though I was shaking.

It wasn't easy, but I kept my promise. Months later I held a ceremony in the Del Close Theater at ImprovOlympic. In front of a crowded room filled with press (that would have put a presidential press conference to shame), I brought out his skull, resting on velvet in a Lucite box. Tony Award winner Robert Falls met me on the stage to accept the behest. To my surprise, Falls opened the box and picked up the skull. What happened next brought tears to my eyes and joy to my heart. I knew it was exactly what Del would have wanted. Falls held out the skull in his right hand and spoke as the eloquent actor he is. "Alas, poor Del, I knew him, Horatio. A man of infinite jest." He continued on, reciting the soliloquy that Del wanted for his skull. Del's wish had come true.

Today, Del's skull resides at the Goodman Theatre in Chicago. His ashes are on a special altar that honors him at the ImprovOlympic in the Del Close Theater—where he can affect the work. His thoughts and teachings are being spread around the world.

Melanie Blue was brought in a week after Del's memorial service, and she did indeed eat a vial of his ashes during the Armando Diaz show on a Monday evening, as Del had asked. It's an event that people still ask about.

ImprovOlympic is now a comedy empire with theaters in Chicago and Los Angeles. And Del was right. We have created a "theater of the heart." When people cherish one another on stage night after night, that can't help but form bonds that turn into lasting friendships. ImprovOlympic has become a giant family where people treat one another like geniuses, poets, and artists. Del said that if we treated one another that way, we had a better chance of becoming those kinds of people. That was his way.

Del and I were partners for nineteen years. Old cronies who knew him before I arrived on the scene were amazed to see that he was clean, living in a decent place, doing plays and movies—and had his own theater to boot. I remember one person saying in amazement, "My God, Close—you've gone sane!" The truth is, he wasn't anywhere near normal, and I didn't want to change him that much. I just tried to keep one of his feet on the ground. He was considered a mad genius, and he was entitled to be different. I knew he wasn't mad—he was right.

There was never a dull moment with Del. He had an unusual outlook on everything. I often thought he was dropped off by aliens who left him for me to take care of. We laughed hysterically together, went to the best restaurants, watched strange movies, and read the best books. He was my mentor, my partner, my brother, my son, and my best friend. Yes, I saved his life, but he made mine.

Del left us with the tools to create great works of art, great comedy, and to be a successful business. I, and the performers who studied with him, continue to teach his methods and spread his word. ImprovOlympic goes on without him. But for me, in truth, it's just not as much fun.

Acknowledgments

On a warm August night in 2003 I stood outside ImprovOlympic, talking with my friend Chris McAvoy. I told him one of my Del stories, and soon the two of us were laughing.

"When are you going to write a damn book?" Chris asked.

I shrugged. I had written three plays, but I didn't know if I had it in me to put together a full book. I couldn't answer Chris as to why I hadn't done it. There wasn't any reason why I hadn't at least tried.

"Well, get off your ass and do it," he challenged.

That night I wrote the first chapter. I thank Chris for pushing me to put this book in motion.

Homer Marrs and Marla Caceres were essential in helping me edit the book. Homer helped me with the first draft while Marla took on major parts of the first draft and all the later drafts. Gail Lyman also edited several chapters that needed immediate attention, and was an immense help in finding a publisher. She was always full of encouragement and support. With an office full of people, she screamed, "Holy shit!" when I gave her the news that the book would be published.

Also lending valuable support were Julie Kerber, Melissa Tolheizen, Mike Loeffelholz, Sammy Tamimi, Jeannie Cahill, Jason Chin, and Carla Wold. As a network of friends, they were wonderful advisers. For several hours Julie sat with me as I pored over old newspapers and magazines doing research. She whined constantly and demanded I buy her pizza, but her contribution was mighty.

Steve Schulz and George Eckart supplied me with valuable information that I thought was lost. Bridget Kloss and Rebecca Langguth reminded me of events that took place in our class. Justin Seidner provided me with professional advice, while his father Joel assisted me with legal guidance.

Nate Schaefer immediately called his sister when he was told that I had sent the manuscript to Ivan R. Dee. For that, I'll always be grateful. Thanks to Hilary Meyer for reading the book in one night and then recommending it. I owe Ivan Dee much for publishing the book and for his editorial advice along with some very kind words.

Jeffrey Sweet's, *Something Wonderful Right Away,* and Janet Coleman's *The Compass* were significant resources in my research. Both are great books that provide wonderful insight on Del and Second City.

I would be remiss if I did not thank my family: my parents Dale and Joyce, my sisters Jeni, Melissa, Amy, and Pam, and my brother Jacob. I love them a great deal. Two of my greatest influences growing up were two of my teachers, D. Ann Jones and Jerry Dellinger. They're just as influential now as they were then.

The improv community has been good to me. ImprovOlympic, the Playground, and WNEP have provided me with amazing opportunities. I'm ever so thankful for such wonderful places to play. The Chicago Improv Network was an incredible sounding board during the first couple of months that I began working on this project. Visit them often at www.chicagoimprov.org and you'll find an immediate home where you're accepted no matter what your foibles may be. Cesar Jamie's "Delmonic Interviews" was invaluable and a must-see for improvisers.

Finally, my special thanks to Charna Halpern. It is because

of her that I met Del. After he died, she hired me to teach and work at ImprovOlympic. After she read the book, the two of us discussed it for several hours. She helped me fill in some of the gaps in Del's life and gave me her approval to proceed. She is a good and honest person.

Index

A NOTE ON THE AUTHOR

Jeff Griggs is an actor, director, and improviser in Chicago. Born in Quincy, Illinois, he went to school at Lincoln College, Greenville College, and Illinois State University before starting to work in radio in Decatur, Illinois. He was attracted to improvisational theater because of The Second City group in Chicago, and became a student at ImprovOlympic before embarking on the adventures that comprise this book.